Emma H. (Emma Hildreth) Adams

**To and fro in Southern California**

Emma H. (Emma Hildreth) Adams

**To and fro in Southern California**

ISBN/EAN: 9783741143328

Manufactured in Europe, USA, Canada, Australia, Japa

Cover: Foto ©Andreas Hilbeck / pixelio.de

Manufactured and distributed by brebook publishing software (www.brebook.com)

Emma H. (Emma Hildreth) Adams

**To and fro in Southern California**

LIBRARY OF THE
UNIVERSITY OF ILLINOIS
AT URBANA-CHAMPAIGN

917.94
Ad1t

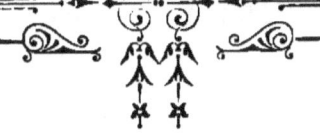

# TO AND FRO

IN

# Southern California.

WITH

SKETCHES IN ARIZONA AND NEW MEXICO.

BY

## EMMA H. ADAMS,

Author of "Digging the Top Off," and other Stories.

CINCINNATI:
W. M. B. C. PRESS.
1887.

# PREFACE.

THIS little volume consists of a series of letters written to certain Eastern journals—chiefly to the Cleveland "Leader and Herald"—from Southern California, during the year 1884 and a few weeks in the Autumn of 1886. The writer has chosen to present them in chapters, rather than in the form of letters. In a few chapters the letters of the earlier and later sojourn have been mingled, in some instances, at the expense of perfect clearness as to the time. This the writer regrets, but having strong reasons, thought best to adopt this plan.

From its nature, the book is in but slight sense a *guide* to persons visiting Southern California, although its pages embrace much reliable information about the country and its people. Still, so rapid are the changes which take place on this part of the coast, that what was true of it in 1884, and even last year, may not be true of it to-day. The writer has aimed to build, out of the many sketches and facts given, a pleasant and readable book. That the work is free from errors she dare not affirm.                                         E. H. A.

# CONTENTS.

| CHAPTER. | | PAGE. |
|---|---|---|
| I. | WESTWARD BOUND, | 9 |
| II. | THE SOUTHWARD RUN, | 16 |
| III. | ITS TO-DAY AND YESTERDAY, | 20 |
| IV. | OLD TIMES AND PRESENT RESOURCES, | 26 |
| V. | THE CHURCH AND SCHOOL-HOUSE ARE THE PIONEERS, | 33 |
| VI. | INCIDENTS OF THE SECOND JOURNEY, | 38 |
| VII. | FROM DEMING TO TUCSON, | 44 |
| VIII. | ARIZONA, | 49 |
| IX. | TUCSON, | 55 |
| X. | FROM TUCSON TO LOS ANGELES, | 58 |
| XI. | THE CITY OF LOS ANGELES, | 62 |
| XII. | INVALIDS IN SOUTHERN CAIFORNIA, | 73 |
| XIII. | WHAT SHALL WE WEAR? | 82 |
| XIV. | A FORMER HOME OF GENERAL AND MRS. HANCOCK, | 86 |
| XV. | CALIFORNIA'S GREAT HISTORIAN, | 94 |
| XVI. | AN ILL WIND THAT BLEW GOOD, | 107 |
| XVII. | A SINGULAR CHARACTER, | 122 |
| XVIII. | THE NATIVE CALIFORNIANS, | 131 |
| XIX. | SCHOOLS OF LOS ANGELES, | 139 |
| XX. | A NOBLE PIONEER, | 150 |

## CONTENTS.

| CHAPTER. | | PAGE. |
|---|---|---|
| XXI. | COLONIZATION SCHEMES, | 170 |
| XXII. | VINEYARDS AND ORANGE GROVES, | 187 |
| XXIII. | THE PICOS AND THE SURRENDER OF CAHUENGA, | 200 |
| XXIV. | TIME BEGUILES YOU, | 210 |
| XXV. | A MINISTER TO THE LOWLIEST, | 217 |
| XXVI. | ROSES — PAMPAS GRASS — THE DATURA ARBOREA, | 227 |
| XXVII. | WOMEN AS CULTIVATORS OF THE SOIL, | 236 |
| XXVIII. | SAN PEDRO, | 246 |
| XXIX. | IN THE SANTIAGO CANON, | 257 |
| XXX. | A WONDERFUL FLOWER FESTIVAL, | 267 |
| XXXI. | FROM LOS ANGELES TO SAN FRANCISCO, | 277 |

# TO AND FRO

IN

# SOUTHERN CALIFORNIA.

## I.

### WESTWARD BOUND.

SOON after dark of a cold December night, 1883, a carriage containing three persons, the writer being one, whirled rapidly over the glistening, snow-covered pavement toward the great Union Depot in C——. Two of us had begun the journey to the far-off Pacific coast. The third occupant, after the good-bye and the parting, was to return alone into the city.

Of us who were westward bound, one was very ill, and, as it proved, was in a double sense hastening towards the sunset.

Soon we were nicely settled in the luxurious sleeper. Around us stood a gratifying array of boxes and baskets, which loving hands had packed with delicacies for the invalid and substantial provisions for the other.

Time sped, and when the clock opposite the train indicated the hour for starting, but two of us were left on board. The wheels began to turn. A man took the cards off the cars and walked away. Then out of the noisy building we rolled, into star-light and snow-light. On we went, past hamlet, and town, and farm, until, soon after sunrise the second morning, we rumbled into Kansas City.

Then took place those agreeable little episodes of the trans-continental journey; the transferring ourselves to the shining Pullman of the Atchison, Topeka, and Santa Fe railway, the weighing and re-checking of baggage, and the taking breakfast. This all done, we glided off across the broad, liberty-loving State of Kansas. Bare and desolate as were the famous plains at that season, they were made intensely interesting by the thrilling experiences they recalled, connected with overland traveling in an early day. Dashing along at a rapid rate, well protected from the dust and cold, and as comfortable as if in a parlor, how faintly we realized the depressing tediousness of toiling over those dreary stretches behind a slow ox-team!

Armed cap-a-pie were most of those early adventurers into the wilds of the West, with patience, hope, and courage. That is a curious and startling element in human nature, which leads men to face danger from choice; to push out from comfort into hardship; away from privilege into privation. But so have men again and again followed the Star of Empire around the world.

The sight of a vast plain, as of a great mountain, leaves a deep impression upon the mind. Both suggest the possession of mighty power by the Architect of the world. As to that, power always impresses us, be it lodged in the winds, in steam, in the little plant forcing its way. out of the soil, or in the Creator's hand, lifting the rocks up into mountains, or rolling millions of acres out into plains, level as a floor.

As we approached the western verge of the State, the country became first undulating, then hilly, and as we neared the border of Colorado it began to stand upright, while far in the west snow-capped summits appeared. It was a new thing to be able to see objects eighty miles distant, as an *attaché* of our shining car affirmed were some of the snow-cones of the Greenhorn Range.

Running on to La Junta, Colorado, where the

road makes a decided turn towards the south, we soon had a fine view of the summit of Pike's Peak, declared by the conductor to be one hundred and fifty miles to the northward. Suddenly foot-hills, clothed with snow and cedars, sprang up all around us. Then our train began to climb, the upward tendency of our course being very perceptible. We were pushing on towards the Raton Pass, in the mountains of that name.

On our right about this time, were discovered the majestic Spanish Peaks, three cones, snow-tipped and looming up finely. Arrived at the base of the rugged Raton Range, the strength of our one engine was insufficient to carry us up to the tunnel through which the road crosses the summit. Accordingly, "Uncle Ned," one of the largest locomotives in the United States, and certainly a mighty fellow, was marched to the front to "lend a hand." And nobly did he perform the task. Sweeping up that steep grade was a splendid piece of climbing. A strong wind blew down the pass into the giant's face. The car in which we rode strained, creaked, and swayed as we went up and up, turning around this shoulder and around that. Several young ladies in the car were in terror, lest Uncle Ned should lose his foot-hold, and let them go rolling down the mountain-side, to become the victims of a second Tehachapi disaster. Happily he was shod for the steep roadway of steel, and no such casualty occurred.

If I am correct, it has been the happy privilege of Uncle Ned to pull up to the tunnel in the Raton Pass, every westward-bound passenger train since the completion of the road to this time. Men become attached to inanimate things, and I was told that the employees of the road have a regard for this engine, much like that a brave general feels for an intelligent horse which has borne him through many a well-fought battle.

On the train, much interested in Uncle Ned's struggle for the ascendency, were Mr. James C. Warner and his wife, of Chicago, bound for Melbourne, Australia. Mr. Warner is an English electrician, and among that class of scientists is known as an able inventor. He goes to the Fifth Continent as the agent of the Western Electric Company, and in the city of Melbourne will superintend the application, to machines already in use, the latest improvements in telephonic apparatus. This company, he informed me, controls the system of telephones now working in that city, and hopes, by promptly attaching thereto every important new appliance, to secure a market for its instruments in other towns of Australia. Mr. Warner has more the air of an unpretending farmer than of a devout student in the realm of electricity.

The boundary line between Colorado and New Mexico runs through the Raton Tunnel, about midway of its length. We crossed this line, eight thousand feet above sea-level, a couple of hours after dark. A sensation of descent, as distinct as that we had experienced of ascent in going up, told us the moment we had passed this confine. This brought us into Colfax County, New Mexico, one of the largest and most promising sections of the Territory. It is a well-known stock region of the South-west. During the night our route lay, first, amid austere mountain scenery, and then across broad mesas and plains.

In the following sketches, which pertain particularly to New Mexico and Arizona, I have mingled the accounts of two trips across the Great American Desert, between which nearly three years intervened. With the exception of a single episode or two, I have so woven these together as to make them read like the observations of one journey, ignoring dates, and endeavoring only to present clearly the facts gleaned. Instead of receiving detriment by the arrangement, it is believed the reader will rather be benefited. Should it appear necessary to introduce a date at any point for the clearer apprehension of the reader, it will be done.

## II.

# THE SOUTHWARD RUN.

### A STAR-ROUTE MAN.

DURING the night we drew up at a small town named "Dorsey," after the famous "Star Route" Senator, now a resident of New Mexico. We had supposed this town to be located not far from Mr. Dorsey's great stock farm. But in this we were mistaken. The next station, called Springer, is the nearer his home, and is the place where he always takes the cars when bound on a visit to the outside world. Mr. Dorsey's immense farm, according to a personal acquaintance of the ex-Senator, riding in the seat next us, lies some thirty miles from the railway. Upon it he is now erecting an expensive and handsome residence, "one staircase in which," said the gentleman, "will cost him seven hundred dollars." Mr. Dorsey is the possessor of large flocks and herds, and, notwithstanding the taint upon his reputation inflicted by the memorable star-route investigation, he exerts some political influence in the Territory.

### ANTELOPE, A WOLF.

While we were speeding over the plains in this county the second time, which was by daylight, some one raised the cry:

"See the antelope! see the antelope!"

And on looking out of the windows we saw a small group of the graceful creatures quietly feeding, a few rods from the train. And not long after, quite as rare a sight was presented, when a savage wolf stalked away from us, over the parched grass. He held his head aloft and appeared as if he did n't care a penny for the comfort of traveling by steam.

### ALBUQUERQUE.

Morning found us at Albuquerque, the largest city in New Mexico, having a population of about ten thousand souls. The place received its name from the Duke of Albuquerque, for four years the Spanish Governor and Captain-general of New Mexico, in the seventeenth century. It is quite noted for the educational advantages it possesses, while, as yet, no efficient system of public schools maintains in the Territory. The Albuquerque Academy is a promising institution, supervised by

Protestants. There is also conducted a Catholic school of considerable strength; while on a farm near the city flourishes the United States Industrial School for Indian Children. To this even juvenile Apaches are admitted without a fear of their getting on the war-path. The school is said to have been modeled after those at Hampton and Carlisle.

As certain evidences of its future growth, the city points to its central location; to the rich valleys lying north and south of it; to its contiguous coal and mineral mines; to its importance as a railroad center, and best of all, to the activity and public spirit of its citizens.

The first objects to arrest attention, on our leaving the train for breakfast, were a dozen or less savage-looking Indians, sitting, standing, lying down, on the broad veranda of the hotel. Men and women were clad in the same costume—heavy woolen blankets wrapped about the shoulders, and thick leggings tied above the knee. The sky was overclouded, and a fierce wind swept every inch of the piazza. Yet there they remained, bronzed statues, silently watching the passengers come and go, until the train pulled out southward. Not the vestige of a smile, or an emotion, lighted up their coarse features. Possibly their thought was:

"What wonderful beings these white-skins are!" And possibly: "What thieves and robbers!" But whatever their opinions, they will be spoken only to one another.

No sooner does one interested in the human race, enter New Mexico, than he becomes curious in regard to certain Indian tribes dwelling in the Territory. By the term "Indian" I mean, not simply wild Red men, but the inhabitants of both American continents when first invaded by Europeans. This includes the nations and tribes of the United States, the peoples whom Cortez subjugated in Mexico and Central America, and the race whom Pizarro overthrew in Peru, all of whom ethnologists now conveniently group together under the term, "the American race." But arousing a profounder curiosity are those earlier peoples, who long preceded the American race, the ruins of whose works are a marvel to-day. Of their mighty builders no reliable account can be given. The very aspect of New Mexico starts trains of thought about those old, old occupants of the land. How long ago they lived, here, in Yucatan, in Peru, no pen can tell. So we turn a leaf and write about the country.

## III.

## ITS TO-DAY AND YESTERDAY.

A MELANCHOLY LAND — NUMEROUS FORMER INHABITANTS — POPULATION TO-DAY — THE PUEBLO INDIANS — THEIR OLD CITIES — MINING OPERATIONS AND SUCCESSFUL FORM OF GOVERNMENT — THE SPANISH INVASION — NEW MEXICO AS NOW CONSTITUTED.

NEW MEXICO is a quaint and singular portion of the United States. Thousands of acres of it are mere dismal stretches of sand. Yet stand where one will, mountain chains enter into the landscape. They push out into the desert in all directions, reckless, apparently, of all law and order; so that it may truly be said: "Everywhere on its surface the extremes of scenery meet." Though a radiant, sunny region, it is yet a strange and lonely land; a land given up to silence and the winds. True, one may not now, as did Antonio de Espejo three hundred years ago, "travel fifteen days in the province without meeting any people;" still, even in this year of grace 1883, and employing the modern mode of progress, one may ride for hours over the desolate wastes and see almost no inhabitants. Occasionally the train dashes past a low adobe hut, far away from any town, but he catches no glimpse of the inmates. There are no faces of children at the little square windows, no forms in the low doorway. The ordinary tokens of civilization, seen all along the great railroads throughout the East, are absent here. Corn fields, wheat fields, and orchards are rare, except near the villages, or in the vicinity of the Rio Grande.

Nevertheless, it must not be inferred that New Mexico is without population. In 1881 it exceeded in number of inhabitants any other territory of the Union, except the District of Columbia. The census of 1880 gave it nearly 121,000 people, the natives being in strongest force. But what seems a little startling, unless one is conversant with the past history of this part of our country, is, that in Espejo's day New Mexico sustained a much greater multitude of people than at present. In the interests of Spain that officer traversed districts which embraced "fourteen, twenty, thirty, and even fifty thousand persons." This was in the northern portion of the province, however, and these communities were assemblages of the Pueblo Indians, a people whom he found to be not only extremely industrious and living peaceably under their caciques, but also possessing many of the luxuries of life, practicing numerous arts of civilization, and exhibiting toward strangers an ungrudging hospitality. A recent report by the Governor of the Territory asserts that ten thousand of these Pueblos now dwell in New Mexico, and offer to the student of ethnology a subject as fascinating as when the Spaniards invaded the land. An intelligent writer upon the times and history of these ancient New Mexicans, says of them, substantially:

"They were a nation who lived permanently in homes, some of them in houses built of stone, five lofts in height. They tilled the soil; constructed irrigating ditches to water their corn fields and gardens; made thoughtful provision against famine; wove cloths; wore painted mantles; had articles of dress embroidered in needle-work; used jewelry made of the turquois, emerald, and garnet; and administered wholesome laws, generations before the landing of Columbus."

New Mexico abounds in legends and folk-lore relating to this race. And the many remains of ancient towns and cities, planted by its members on her hills, plateaus, and desert borders, tell in some degree how they lived and have passed away. Old mines, "caved in and covered up," together with "ruined smelters, surrounded by heaps of imperishable slag," evince their knowledge of the minerals with which the mountains teem. The broken pottery, sacred images, and other domestic relics left by them, have rendered New Mexico a delightful field for the archæologist and antiquarian for nearly a half century past.

A district particularly rich in these ancient tokens is the county of Rio Arriba, in the northwestern part of the territory. Here the traveler finds himself in the old realm of the Cliff Dwellers, where now may be seen the ruins of many of their villages, and where, buried out of sight beneath mounds of slowly accumulated soil, lie numerous others.

"Judging by the depth of the earth above them," says one of the officials of that county, "this people must have settled the country thousands of years ago." Some of their ancient cities were of vast extent. Remains of them exist in the valleys, on the mesas, on the mountains, and far up the sides of rocky cliffs, which present an almost perpendicular front.

But between the era of the prosperous Village

Indians, and the domination of the Americans in New Mexico, there intervened another nation. It came into the country bearing the gospel of peace in one hand and the sword in the other; came in to vanquish, not to uplift and improve. It built royal edifices, "exacting from the hitherto happy Pueblos" slavish and unrequited labor. And not seldom did it inflict upon them the cruel punishments of the Inquisition. By its rapacious policy was begotten, in the course of years, a spirit of revolt and revenge which, in 1680, turned the peaceful province into a scene of furious incendiarism and bloodshed.

Perhaps nowhere on either of the American continents where the Spaniards obtained sway, did they display toward the races they subjugated a greater tyranny, or a more studied treachery, than in the country by themselves called, "The Kingdom and Province of New Mexico," and which then included, besides the New Mexico of our day, the whole of Arizona and a portion of Colorado.

The invasion of the Spaniards took place "about one hundred years before the Pilgrims set foot upon Plymouth Rock." Yet to-day the strong and ornate structures they reared, some in ruins, others in comparatively good preservation, occupy many a vantage ground of the region. Thus one finds here the eloquent works, as well as the living representatives of two former races, both of which have lost control of the country. All this, and more, tends to throw over the Territory of New Mexico a fascination and an air of romance which years will fail to dispel. Indeed, in greater or less degree, the same weird interest is aroused by all this dreamy, desert portion of the United States. The vegetation is unique. A blue haze veils the mountains. The distances deceive. The mirages are illusions.

At the close of the Spanish dominion there succeeded the Mexican régime. This, in turn, was followed by the American occupation in 1848, our Government having acquired New Mexico in that year by the treaty of Guadalupe Hidalgo.

## IV.

## OLD TIMES AND PRESENT RESOURCES.

ITS AREA—CHIEF CITIES—OLD CITY OF SANTA FE—GOVERNOR'S RESIDENCE—OLD CHURCH OF SAN MIGUEL—ROCKY MOUNTAIN MEN—RESOURCES OF THE TERRITORY—PRODUCTS—AND FOUR RIVERS.

NEW MEXICO, as now constituted, contains an area of 121,201 square miles. Its average breadth is three hundred and sixty-seven miles; its average length, three hundred and thirty-five miles. Among the names of its counties we find the illustrious ones of Lincoln, Grant, and Colfax. Its chief cities are Santa Fe, the capital, Albuquerque, already mentioned, and the point at which the Atlantic and Pacific Railway leaves the Atchison, Topeka, and Santa Fe road for San Francisco, Los Vegas, celebrated for its hot springs, Las Cruces, Silver City, Deming, and some others.

In age and historic interest, as well as in legendary charm, Santa Fe, colonized and re-named by the Spaniards in 1598, stands pre-eminent. Probably no other spot in all this lower portion of our land is so rich in old Indian traditions, in memories of the relentless Spanish rule, and in reminiscences of the intrepid Rocky Mountain fur traders. Its plaza, streets, buildings, and some special precincts, are eloquent with the deeds of the three races which have successively held sway there.

Prior to the Spanish settlement, the place was the governing center for a group of Indian villages which were confederated under one cacique, and enjoyed a remarkable prosperity, if we may credit the testimony of their conquerors. These were villages of the gentle "Tanos people," upon whom were executed, after 1662, some of the harsh edicts of the Inquisition.

Among the points of attraction belonging to a former day are the old Church of San Miguel, the Cathedral of San Francisco, Fort Marcy, certain old landmarks of the American fur traders, and the structure called the Governor's Residence. The latter is said to be the oldest, and the only building in the United States, preserved since the Spanish sway, which is distinctively called a palace. It is now familiarly known as the Governor's Residence, and is occupied by the American Governor of the Territory. No single feature of the old city excites more interest in the minds of visitors than does this dwelling.

It is a one-story, adobe structure, with very thick walls, like all such works left by the Spaniards, and is supposed to have been erected by Count Penaloza, chief executive of the province, about 1662. Around it cluster volumes of historical associations. One of its distinctions is the great number of titled people which have been entertained within it, in royal state. Considering its location, in the heart of a great country, and the fact that from no direction could it be reached, except by traversing arid stretches of vast extent, or by crossing mountains rugged and bold, this feature is all the more noteworthy. Among its guests have been envoys of the kings of Spain, Mexican officials, and distinguished citizens of the United States.

Penaloza, so runs the history, possessed not only a decided taste for building cities and fine edifices, but also great tact for quelling Indian outbreaks. At the same time, he was not the man to meekly execute all the decrees of the home government. It is related that on one occasion he laid hold of a Spanish commissary-general and confined him in the palace for a week, in the hope that quietude and time for reflection might teach him official moderation. How he succeeded is not stated.

Modern writers have worked away at the ancient

Church of San Miguel, until most readers know all about it. The principal facts concerning the structure, besides the history wrapped up in it, are the following: It is believed to be the oldest church edifice in the United States. Like scores of similar buildings in Arizona, Old Mexico, and California, it was made of adobe, with walls immensely thick. Its exterior is prison-like. In the general Pueblo emeute of 1680 it suffered partial destruction, but was restored thirty years later.

Near it stands a low adobe structure, two stories in height, "known to antedate every other house in our land," it being the only remains of the ancient Pueblo village, or capital, of Analco, which, at Espejo's advent, occupied the present site of Santa Fe.

In the early years of this century there flourished, at times, in Santa Fe such notable Rocky Mountain men as Kit Carson and Captain Zebulon Pike, whose name is perpetuated by that peerless summit, Pike's Peak, and who once languished, for some little time, a prisoner in the famous "palace." Added to these were Jedediah Smith, the two Soublette brothers, the Messrs. Fitzpatrick and Bridger, besides a score of less eminent but not less fearless traders, trappers, and adventurers, who, in spite of great obstacles and extreme reverses, built up a rich commerce with Northern Mexico.

The resources of New Mexico may be grouped under the heads of grazing, mining, agriculture, as yet carried on to an extent much below the possibilities, horticulture, in which encouraging beginnings have been made, and endless openings for manufactures. Immense herds of cattle, sheep, goats, and horses range over its boundless pasture tracts. A glimpse of these herds is sometimes obtained by the traveler as he flits through the Territory on the cars. Millions of acres are given up to this purpose.

In the mountains of New Mexico lie buried in vast quantities, gold, silver, copper, coal, mica, and numerous other metals. Santa Fe County, embracing the celebrated Cerrillos anthracite fields, twenty thousand acres in extent, together with the Callisteo bituminous banks, of equal size, and those of Socorro County, on the eastern side of the Rio Grande, represent the wealth of a kingdom in fuel alone.

Donna Ana County, one hundred and fifty miles long, one hundred miles wide, lying on the border of Old Mexico and well watered by the Rio Grande, excels in semi-tropical fruit products.

Every thing may be grown there, from apples to strawberries, grown in abundance and to perfection. Onion culture is also a prominent industry of the district. The variety raised is a native of Old Mexico, and has a great reputation for size and fine flavor. In these particulars it surpasses the favorite Bermuda onion. One cultivator of the fragrant (?) edible, says: "An acre of ground will produce thirty thousand onions, averaging one pound in weight, and with skillful husbandry even fifty thousand pounds may be obtained from the same space. The crop may be marketed on the ground at three cents per pound, and will require the steady labor of one man six months of the year.

A conspicuous resource of this county is its gypsum plains, forty miles long by thirty miles wide. The mineral exists in the form of powder, and in some localities is "piled in drifts, from twenty to fifty feet in height." From a distance, it is said, these ridges resemble banks of snow. Its special value lies in its being a fine fertilizer for wheat.

Four great rivers, with many lesser streams, water the Territory of New Mexico. The Rio Grande and the Rio Picos flow through its entire length, from north to south, and find their outlet in the Gulf of Mexico. The latter is the more eastern stream, and refreshes Lincoln County, an immense area, embracing about one-fifth of the Territory.

Rio Arriba County is another mammoth section. Its altitude above sea-level averages seven thousand feet. Its length is two hundred and fifty miles, its width ninety miles. Through it flows the river San Juan, a strong affluent of the Colorado, and having many large branches of its own.

Turning now to the north-eastern corner of the Territory, we behold rolling into populous San Miguel County, from Texas, the Canadian River, an important arm of the Arkansas. With its own multiplied tributaries it nourishes a fine series of fertile valleys. In this section the hills and mountain slopes bristle with forests of pine and cedar. On the streams are numerous saw-mills, busy cutting this timber into lumber, thus adding another to the resources of New Mexico.

## V.

## THE CHURCH AND SCHOOL-HOUSE ARE THE PIONEERS.

EDUCATION IN THE BROAD WEST—PUEBLO WOMEN—OLD SANTA FE TRAIL—A NEW MEXICAN SUNSET—VENUS.

BEFORE resuming the thread of my story, after this long digression, I wish to make one or two remarks on the subject of general education in this and other south-western parts of our country, and to make them in connection with Wallace, the terminus of a division of the Atchison, Topeka, and Santa Fe Railway, where are located the company's shops, round-house, and the like. Wallace is a point of interest, also, on account of the liberal provision it has made for the education and religious culture of its people, and in these respects it is a typical Western town. It is not unusual in these towns to find the church and school-house going up simultaneously with the dwellings. Indeed, in my journeyings I have seen a town-site on which a church, a school-house, and a hotel were among the first buildings erected, and the men laying out the place were of the shrewdest, most far-seeing class. Another preliminary step was the grading of the principal streets and the laying of durable pavements. Then followed electric lights, and the next thing was a railway train thundering in.

It has been reserved for the West, the undefined but prodigious West, to reverse the order of proceedings in founding towns and cities. The old plan was for a number of families to appear, one by one, on the scene, erect their habitations and get settled at their various pursuits. Then tardily followed the church edifices and the institutions of learning. Now the latter are the pioneers. They move on, in advance of the people, take possession of the ground, and are ready to begin work when the men and women, the boys and girls, come up.

Now returning to our journey: We were some three hours beyond Albuquerque, when, halting at a station in the desert, our car was invaded by a band of Pueblo women carrying baskets of "pinions," a small nut gathered on the neighboring mountains, and which resembled a variety of brown bean I have frequently seen in Ohio. The fruit was sweet and pleasant to the taste, and was offered us at five cents the tumbler full. These little women were a lively company, and flitted to and fro in the car, disposing of their nuts in a very brisk, business-like manner. They were clad in indescribable attire, and evidently in expectation of seeing strangers. Each woman wore upon her head about the following articles: A square piece of colored cloth, a gay handkerchief, and a sun-bonnet tied with cord and tassels. The remainder of the costume was similarly varied, both as to garments and color. There could be little question but that each one had donned her entire wardrobe for the occasion. With their coal-black eyes, alert ways, and pleasant expression of countenance, they were agreeable women, notwithstanding their swarthy skin, short stature, and stout bodies.

## THE OLD SANTA FE TRAIL.

Not far to the east of us now, through many miles of the treeless desert, lay the celebrated Santa Fe Trail, formerly pursued by emigrants on their way to the great El Dorado of the West.

"For a distance of ninety miles through New Mexico," said a gentleman familiar with the Territory, "this route crossed not a single stream of running water; and to this part of it was given the name of 'Valley of Death.' And such, indeed, it was.

Great numbers of men and animals fell victims to thirst upon its suffocating sands."

Here and there the precise locality of the trail was pointed out to us, as we sped down the desolate expanse.

Many of the small hamlets which have sprung up because the railroad is here, are as quiet and dreamy as the desert itself. No business is transacting. No hum of manufacturing is heard. No teams are at work. Not a woman is seen abroad in the streets. No child voices ring out through the heated air. And yet this is sunny New Mexico, a land which many people who have not traversed it, suppose to be clothed with verdure, radiant with flowers, and teeming with inhabitants.

It was a relief, under the circumstances, to have the long, bright day wear away, and to see the sun go down. Suddenly, thereupon, fully one-quarter of the great arch overhead turned to a brilliant gold color. Half-way up to the zenith this softened into a faint pink, while at the horizon it deepened to a rich orange. Soon after, in the midst of the gold, appeared the fair evening star, its soft, silvery beams contrasting strikingly with the glory around. Slowly, then, night dropped her

## ALBUQUERQUE. 37

curtains, now concealing this range of mountains, and now that. It was nine o'clock. We were in Deming, the south-western terminus of the Atchison and Topeka road.

The only hotel was crowded with guests, waiting for a delayed train on the Southern road. Not a room remained for the passengers from the North. Happily, between the proprietor and a housekeeper across the plaza there existed a silent partnership in the hotel business, which was made apparent on such occasions. To her house, accordingly, were we marched, an inhospitable wind chilling us to our very bones. Arrived at the place, we were conducted up an outside staircase to our rooms, in none of which was sign of fire, beyond a warm stove-pipe, which passed through one of them from below. This was kindly assigned to the sufferer in my care, and in a short time weariness and desert solitudes were forgotten in sound sleep.

## VI.

## INCIDENTS OF THE SECOND JOURNEY.

NEARLY three years after that night I again passed over this section of New Mexico, and if the reader will pardon, I will insert here, before we move westward from Deming, one or two episodes of that trip.

Under my care, by her own request, was an aged German woman, for long years a resident of San Francisco. So singular a character was she, such a compound of smartness and utter inability, so unattractive in appearance, and yet so winning withal, that I presume to photograph her on these pages.

Upon entering the Pullman car at Los Angeles, I found her domiciled for the trip, and conversing with a couple of genteel-looking friends. The berth I had secured happened to be opposite her own. Presently her friends bade her "good-bye," and we were alone. Then turning to me she remarked:

"May be you are going where I am?"

"Possibly. I am going to Ohio."

"Is that east of Medora, Kansas?"

"Yes, a long distance."

"May be, then, you'll look after me. I've never been over this road before. I live in San Francisco—thirty years now in that wonderful city."

"I will, certainly, do all I can for you."

Then she proceeded to epitomize her austere history, by saying that she had been a hard worker all her days; had made and lost two or three ample fortunes; had buried her husband two years before; had been left childless, and now, tired of a silent home and a desolate life, she had started for Medora, Kansas, "expressly to take back with her a favorite niece and her family, to brighten the house."

"Should they prove kind to her," she went on, "and not be too stuck up, the step should be the making of them. But should they forget the respect due her, they'd just have to pack up and git. And, in that event, she should just take up the dead body of her husband and git to Europe. Germany was a better place, anyhow, than this wretched, sandy country."

Hundreds of miles before reaching Deming, she became disgusted with the route, and "just wished she'd gone by the Union Pacific. That was a wonderful route, through magnificent scenery. But on this Southern Pacific road she'd seen nothing but sand, mountains, and twisted cacti for nearly thirteen hundred miles; and, what was worse yet, the attendant in the car assured her there were twelve hundred miles more of the same thing before she would see Medora." Thus the good woman vented her discontent upon the innocent country.

It was a singular aspect of her case that, untidy as was her appearance, coarse as were her manners and features, she yet managed to interest in her behalf every traveler who happened to take seat near her. On leaving the car, men and women would shake hands with her warmly, wishing her a safe arrival at "Medora," and success with the niece and her family. To the through passengers this proceeding became rather amusing toward the last. At the same time it disclosed a beautiful side of our human nature.

An important part of the woman's luggage consisted of a capacious portmanteau, crowded with such fragrant provisions as pickles, cheese, ham, doughnuts, and bologna sausage. From either one of these the odor could have been endured; but when all had been combined and confined for several hours, they had the effect to set her near neighbors to devising an emigration scheme the moment the receptacle was opened. From this supply, with the addition of a cup of coffee, procured for her at the meal stations, she refreshed herself three times each day. Though twice and a half my weight, she seemed to regard me as a being who could avert from her all the evils of the way, and, indeed, but for my oversight on leaving Deming, the poor woman would have been doomed to spend twenty-four hours more in that "horrid sandy country."

At half-past nine in the morning we were located in the cool, wicker-seated coaches, ready for the flight northward. Toward noon we came in sight of the green fringe of the Rio Grande. Crossing this stream we soon drew up at Rincon, a place consisting of the station-house and a very comfortable hotel. Both are shoved up into a narrow cañon, in order to escape overflows of the great river. Here, during a three hours' waiting for the northward-bound train from El Paso, we witnessed a striking display of the mental resources of the Mexican in times of emergency, and also of his capacity to sympathize with others in condition of suffering.

Soon after our arrival one of their race attempted, when in a state of intoxication, to leap upon an incoming local train. One of the brakemen, perceiving the man's danger, pushed him away vigorously. Enraged by this act, the crazed fellow repeated the effort, missed his hold, fell beneath the car, and was taken up with one foot severely crushed. He became sober instantly.

Lying about on blankets, bedding, and bundles of apparel in the broad covered passage-way between the two trains, were a score of his countrymen, unmoved by the accident and indifferent to the victim's pain. There being no physician within miles of the place, the wounded man was laid on the floor of this passage, without sign of pillow, and freely dosed with whisky, while upon the mangled foot was poured a stream of cold water. Meanwhile, did he attempt to turn his head, to move an arm, or toss about in his agony, his two companions held him as rigid as a statue, regardless of his woeful cry of "Let me alone."

Distressed by all this, several gentlemen, leaving the cars, urged gentler treatment and the pressing need of a surgeon. But the brown-visaged men replied only by a shake of the head, and a few words uttered in the Spanish tongue. The ministration of whisky and water continued during the three hours of our stay, and when we moved off northward the sufferer still lay on the floor, his foot bleeding but himself quiet and unconscious of pain, because dead drunk.

Shortly before four o'clock of the fifth day after our departure from Los Angeles, the polite conductor of the train entered our car, stepped to the seat occupied by my German friend, and said, smilingly, "The next station is Medora," and then passed on. How the good woman's hands trembled then as she tied her bonnet strings, clasped her reticule, and gave the half-dozen pieces of her luggage a quick little shove together to have them ready for a prompt departure! Stepping to her side I said: "Do not worry; I will help you off the train."

Then she calmed herself some and waited, and finally, grateful for her cordial invitation to visit her the next time I should be in "that wonderful city, San Francisco," I bade her "good-bye" in the long-looked-for Medora, and continued my flight toward the Buckeye State.

## VII.

## From Deming to Tucson.

NOW let us return to Deming. The reader will remember we entered the place at nine o'clock in the evening. The next morning, which dawned cold and gray, revealed a small village of possibly sixteen hundred inhabitants. In the distance, on every hand, rose mountains blue and stately. Most of the buildings were of wood, one story in height, and erected, evidently, to serve only until better structures should take their place. The commodious hotel, hemmed in on three sides by railroads, was new and well managed. Its bill of fare was surprisingly ample, and the cooking excellent, for a table spread in the heart of a desert.

Some towns seem to have been foreordained to become eminent. Reputation attaches to them independently of size or age. Location alone secures it to them. This is Deming's prime advantage. The village stands in the path of the ever-increasing tide of travel from the vast "East" to our southwestern coast. Through it pass, also, from the

Pacific Slope thousands of people ticketed to Texas and the Gulf States, while multitudes branch off here for all points east of the Rocky Mountains. Hence the little town is known far and near.

Deming is located about forty miles north of the border of Old Mexico, and is a distributing point for a large region of country. Its altitude above sea-level is four thousand two hundred feet. Underneath the place, some fifty feet below the surface, lies an inexhaustible supply of excellent water. This advantage the citizens naturally set forth with some eloquence, situated as they are, on a great desert unrefreshed by running streams. Like millions of acres of this Southland, the region needs water only to render it marvelously productive, they tell us. The general cultivation of the soil here, however, is much a question of the future. Many of the mountains around are vast store-houses for valuable metals and minerals.

Deming calls itself the half-way station between Kansas City and San Francisco, being twelve hundred miles from the former, and nearly thirteen hundred from the latter. The Southern Pacific Railway connects the place with both the Pacific and Gulf coasts. It is likewise the southern terminus for the narrow-gauge road now finished to

Silver City, situated in a rich mineral region. Proceeding westward as far as Benson, an important mining town of Arizona, Deming has an outlet *via* the Sonora Railway to the port of Guaymas, on the Gulf of California.

At half-past ten we again pushed out into the sand, with two hundred and twenty miles between us and Tucson, Arizona. All day long we rolled over the wild waste, our relation to the mountain chains on either hand, changing every hour. The vegetation of the desert proved an interesting study. At one little station I observed, to my surprise, the Salix Babylonica growing in a hot depression, where one would suppose no green thing could live. I noticed, also, in addition to several strange varieties, frequent large patches of the cactus commonly called "prickly pear," or the cactus opuntia. Here the plant was dwarfed in size and the leaves grew close to the ground.

But afterwards, in the city of Los Angeles, I saw it attain a height of fifteen or eighteen feet. The trunk was bare of limbs to a height of eight or ten feet, while the top of ungainly, distorted branches spread out in all directions. The last time I passed this cactus tree, the edge of each pulpy leaf had burst out into a circlet of yellowish-red blossoms, making it a conspicuous object in the neighborhood. The fruit of this species is not only edible, but palatable, and being round at both ends, reminds one of the short, smooth variety of cucumber, though the color is a lighter green.

When crossing this desert the second time, I was favored with a sight of that strange optical illusion, the mirage. Happening to glance out of the car-window, in the direction of the south-west, about four o'clock in the afternoon, lo! there appeared a broad, placid river flowing through the sand. Inverted in its depths we could plainly see the summits of the nearest mountains, and also the tops of the tallest shrubs close at hand. At one point the stream appeared to divide, and encircle the base of a stately butte standing far away, thus forming an inverted conical island.

"Why! is that a river?" inquired a passenger, springing to her feet, and trying to obtain a clearer view of the scene.

"No, madam," answered the conductor, just then passing through the car. "There is no water within two hundred miles of here."

But again we have digressed. It is not easy to combine in one account the observations of opposite trips through a land like this. On we fly, past acres of cacti and chaparral, towards the quaint old city of Tucson. Once more it is night. The sun sinks behind the low indigo hills, rimming the horizon in the west. The heavens are glorious half-way to the zenith. The stars glitter in the azure sky. The air grows cold, making necessary the fire glowing in the huge stove. Now a passenger steps to the door, looks out ahead, returns, shrugs his shoulders, and announces, "Tucson is in sight."

Presently the train halted in front of an excellent hotel, kept by a family named Porter, whom the writer has occasion long to remember, for kindnesses shown her. Delivering up the checks for our luggage, we stepped into an omnibus and drove into the queer old town for a ten days' sojourn and rest. Some little opportunity occurred during our stay, to acquaint myself with Arizona and its ancient capital Certain general facts gained, appear in the following chapter.

## VIII.

## ARIZONA.

ITS SURFACE — RIVERS — ARCHÆOLOGICAL REMAINS — INDIAN TRIBES — AND MINING RESOURCES.

ARIZONA, once a part of New Mexico, embraces a territory of sixteen thousand square miles. Superficially it consists of deserts, plateaus, valleys, and mountains. Chains of the latter traverse it in almost every direction, with much rich, productive land intervening. The southern portion is an extensive plain, but slightly elevated above the sea. Other parts attain altitudes of from six to nine thousand feet. The splendid cone of Saint Francis towers to a distance of eleven thousand feet. The Rio Colorado is the most notable stream of the Territory, and forms a considerable part of its western boundary. Next in importance is the Gila. Having its source in New Mexico, it flows entirely across the southern portion of Arizona, and joins the Colorado about one hundred and sixty miles north of the Gulf of California. Narrow, swift, and shallow most of the year, it swells to a mighty torrent during the rainy season.

The valley of the Gila appears to have been the seat, not only of a large Spanish colonization, but also of a dense Indian population, far anterior to the Spanish occupation. Portions of it are dotted with the ruins of ancient pueblos and structures of solid masonry, "which seem to have remained untenanted for centuries." There exist evidences of long irrigating canals and other eloquent tokens of a busy, industrial life. Some archæologists have conjectured that a people numbering not less than one hundred thousand, dwelt in the valley of the Gila, hundreds of years before Hernando Cortez ever saw Mexico.

The Rio Colorado is navigable several hundred miles above the Gulf of California. At one point, as all the world has read, its deep, resistless current has plowed a cañon, surpassing in the majesty of its scenery even the famous gorge of the Columbia, itself renowned for grand and awe-inspiring sights. The writer will carry in mind to the end of life some of the wonders which mark that rent in the Cascade Mountains, made by the mighty Columbia. The walls of that portion of the Colorado, called the Grand Cañon, attain a perpendicular height of seven thousand feet.

## THE INDIAN TRIBES.

Arizona still retains a large Indian population. The tribes which live in general amity with the Americans are the Pimas, Yumas, Mojaves, Maricopas, Papagoes, and some others. The Apaches, as the newspapers have taken some pains to say, are notably fierce and hostile. The friendly tribes are more or less engaged in farming, stock-raising, and similar pursuits, parts of the Territory being admirably adapted to these purposes.

## THE MINING INDUSTRY.

With most other classes of the people mining appears to be the leading industry. The mountains teem with valuable metals and minerals. Gold, silver, and copper are the most plentiful. Then follows a long list, useful in the arts, and in a thousand ways helpful to man.

The subject of mining certainly forms the staple for conversation in Tucson, both in the home and on the street. In it women appear to be as deeply interested as men, and numbers of them spend weeks of time every year superintending the development of mines; while others, at great sacrifice of domestic enjoyment, leave their homes and reside in the rude camps months in succession, in order that the members of their families engaged in "working claims" may have the restraints and attractions of home life thrown around them.

As I pen these lines there is loading up in the sunny court of this rambling adobe house, a rough-looking, muddy-wheeled vehicle, in which a young man and his mother, a most interesting woman, are about to set out for a mine they own, something like a hundred miles from Tucson. Upon this mine, within a limited time, according to law, must be performed a specified amount of work, else the claim will be forfeited. The mother and son are to set forth this morning to meet this requirement. They came into the city three days ago, from mining property belonging to the family in another direction. On that claim the husband, mother, and son are making a home, until, as the woman remarked to me, "a wasted fortune could be repaired." Within seventy-five miles of her temporary mining home, not another woman resides!

Such are some of the sacrifices imposed by the struggle for gold and silver in these mountains. Sooner or later the precious ores cost the possessor all they are worth. Usually the road is long before a claim becomes remunerative, even if it prove a remarkably rich one. Great patience, perseverance, and courage, as well as a practical knowledge of mining, and a large outlay of money, are the preface to success. And often, after the lavish expenditure of all these, success hides out of sight.

It has been estimated that from twenty-five to forty per cent of the attempts to extract fortunes from the heart of these mountains end in ruin. The outlay is continual. The income may never come. Far surer of coaxing gold out of the valleys is the man who plants potatoes and corn therein. Still, Arizona is one of the richest mineral lands of the world. Leaving gold and silver out of the question, it is affirmed that the Territory's annual yield of copper alone will in a few years reach the vast sum of twenty-five million dollars. Statistics showing the enormous output of some of the Arizona copper mines might here be given, were it my purpose to cumber this little book with details of that character. I may add here, however, that in the opinion of a thoughtful observer of the industry, both here and in Colorado, "mining, properly conducted, is one of the most remunerative pursuits which men follow, and is excelled in this respect only by the liquor traffic." He might have continued: "There is this marked difference, though, in the getting started. Frequently the miner invests a fortune before he receives a farthing in return. On the other hand, ten dollars will establish a saloon. And not unlikely, the first day after the screen is adjusted inside the front door, revenue from the modest stock of mingled water, chemicals, and alcohol begins to flow in freely."

## IX.

## TUCSON.

ITS LOCATION—AGE—INHABITANTS—AND INTERESTING POINTS.

THE city of Tucson stands in the center of a wide sandy plain, a part of the great desert we have traversed two days and two nights. It lies on the Santa Cruz River, sixty miles north of the frontier of Old Mexico, two hundred and twenty miles west of Deming, two hundred and fifty miles east of Yuma, reputed to be the "hottest place in the world." Tucson is in size the chief town of Arizona, and has a population of about fourteen thousand. Prior to the American *régime* it was a Mexican military post of some consequence. It is now a mining center of much influence, and is the capital of Pima County, itself large enough to make a good-sized state.

Tuscon, like St. Augustine, is an un-American, and, on a small scale, extremely cosmopolitan city. A resident of the place avers that on its streets may be heard eighteen different languages. Americans, Mexicans, Germans, Russians, Italians, Austrians, Frenchmen, Spaniards, Greeks, the Chinese,

Japanese, Portuguese, the African, Irishman, and Sandwich Islander are all here, being drawn to the spot by the irresistible mining influence.

In 1694 the Spaniards established a military station here, for the defense of their Mission of San Xavier. But its Indian occupation antedates that day. So, under cloudless skies, and in sight of haze-mantled mountains, the place has dreamed away the years for centuries past. It contains a few modern dwellings, but the majority are built of adobe, in the style prevalent throughout this region from an early day. Usually they stand flush upon the sidewalk, are one story in height, have the floors laid upon the ground, and, exteriorly, are but straight white walls, pierced for doors and windows. Two or three live newspapers find plenty to do extolling the town, the climate, and the buried wealth of the territory. There are several Protestant churches, with, of course, a Catholic house of worship, and at least two good hotels, the one at the railway station being owned by the Southern Pacific Company.

At one side of this hotel is fenced in a pretty green inclosure, set with trees, shrubs, and unique cacti. On my homeward trip the train halted here for dinner, the Pullman car stopping just in front of this gem of green.  Lazily leaning against the fence, like so many towers of Pisa, were a dozen bronzed Mexicans, who spent the twenty minutes of our stay gazing dreamily at the coaches.  Alone among them stood a tall, handsome young woman, dressed in black, except that over her head was thrown a white shawl of gauzy texture, which fell in folds around her shoulders.  With one elbow resting on the fence, and her eyes fixed upon the engine breathing heavily in front of the train, she remained still as a statue until the sharp clang of the bell, as we moved off, roused her from her musings.  That maiden was the Past of Arizona personified.  It needed the shrill bell and piercing shriek of the locomotive to break up the chronic reverie of the Territory.

Within a few miles of Tucson is to be seen the ancient church of San Xavier, in a state of partial ruin.  Considering the period in which it was reared, and the almost insuperable difficulties overcome in conveying materials to the spot, the work is a wonder.  Reader, in making your visit to the Pacific coast, visit the structure if you can.

## X.

## FROM TUCSON TO LOS ANGELES.

CANDLE-LIGHTING, December 18th, found us again aboard the cars, bound for Los Angeles. The train, heavily loaded with passengers hastening to the sunny clime, was due on the coast next day at sunset. All night we coursed over the desert, a welcome rain laying the dust toward morning. Daybreak greeted us at Yuma, the half-way point.

Yuma may be imagined as a small town, lying on the Colorado, just above the entrance of the Gila. The place is scarcely more inviting than the desert itself. As usual, the houses are made of adobe chiefly. Mexicans are the more numerous class of inhabitants; and the climate, extremely mild in Winter, is insufferably hot in Summer. A fort in the vicinity is garrisoned by a small detachment of United States troops; and decidedly startling, it is said, are the adjectives the soldiers sometimes employ to express the high temperature which prevails in the place a good share of the time.

Yuma is the capital of a district of Arizona,

once occupied by the Indian nation so called. Over a century ago this tribe numbered above three thousand persons, who styled themselves "Sons of the River." History designates them as being at that time a strong, sensible, and energetic race. To-day the case may be differently stated. Only a few years ago the Yumas counted but nine hundred and thirty souls, and every one of them was a wreck physically.

There is still a day's ride before us, and all the morning there is a genuine charm in the fantastic vegetation of the desert, and the more so, as it is refreshed by the falling rain. After some hours we enter the San Gorgonio Pass, in the mountains of that name, and when at the summit have attained the highest elevation between Deming and Los Angeles. The next step is to strike out upon the great mesa which skirts for a distance of eighty miles, probably, the base of the rugged Sierra Madre Mountains, in full view now on our right, until we enter the city. Of this plain more will be said in a subsequent chapter.

From this onward the stations become more frequent. Flowers, carpets of thick, green grass, and new varieties of ornamental trees, attract us at all of them. San Bernardino, located a few miles off the railway toward the north, is the first name with which we are familiar. Carriages are in waiting to convey passengers thither, as the train draws up at the little "outlet station" for the place. San Bernardino is one of the many health resorts of Southern California which are growing in reputation. Its warm springs and peculiar climate render it an especially propitious locality for the victims of rheumatism.

We next hear of Riverside, distinctively a center for raisin culture. To this expanding industry and to the place itself we shall devote a succeeding chapter. As we approach Colton, a rapidly growing town, and now important as the point where the "California Southern" intersects the Southern Pacific Railway, Riverside lies nine miles to the south-east of us.

At five o'clock in the afternoon our train landed its freight of human beings, trunks, and carpet-bags at the depot in Los Angeles. Here we were to tarry but four days and then urge our way into the Valley of the Ojai, lying ninety miles north of the city, and reputed to be "the healthiest spot on the globe." Rain having fallen most of the day, the streets of Los Angeles were narrow seas of mud. And although the sun beamed out brightly just then the atmosphere was chilly. We shivered in our warmest wraps. The question was: Are we really in Southern California, the land of radiance and even temperature, of which we have heard so much? It was hardly just to let the first hour decide.

Driving immediately to the St. Charles Hotel, to whose kindly and sympathetic manager we bore letters of introduction, we were at once made comfortable with a warm room and an appetizing supper—I'm too old-fashioned to call the six o'clock evening meal, dinner. Probably I shall get used to it, for that is the name it goes by, at all the first-class hotels, in this nineteenth century. That "it is not in man that walketh to direct his steps," soon became sadly evident to us. The four days lengthened to eleven. For one of us they were days of pain and suffering. For the other they were crowded with anxiety and watching. When they were passed, the sufferer had fallen asleep until the end comes. A few days later he was laid away, among strange dead, on a gentle hill-slope, facing the sunset. Then the survivor took up this pen.

## XI.

## THE CITY OF LOS ANGELES.

THE city of Los Angeles, four years ago, well known to but comparatively few persons living east of the Mississippi, appeared to have just wakened from its century-long slumber, and to have entered upon a career of amazing prosperity. The Southern Pacific Railroad had been completed between two and three years previously, and now formed, with the Atchison, Topeka and Santa Fe road, a highway of steel across the formidable Great American Desert. By these instrumentalities a toilsome and dangerous journey, requiring months for its accomplishment, had been shortened to a pleasant and every way comfortable, though somewhat monotonous, ride of about three days. The effect was magical. Thousands of people from all over the region east of the Rocky Mountains began pouring into Southern California, the city of Los Angeles being the center from which they radiated to everywhere, ferreting out the lovely nooks for homes, and the eligible situations for farms and towns. Thus was the old Spanish city, together with the thousand charming hills and vales surrounding it, aroused to a new and marvelously vigorous life.

The unwholesome, one-story adobe houses, once the only style seen in the city, and still numerous in the portion termed "Sonora-town," or the Mexican quarter, were fast disappearing, and in their stead were rising tasteful frame dwellings for residences, and durable brick structures for stores and business houses. The population of the place did not greatly exceed twenty thousand, and was a mixture of many nationalities. In the next three years the number of its inhabitants nearly doubled, and now, February, 1887, it claims forty thousand citizens, a note received from there to-day, certifying to that effect.

Four causes, mainly, have promoted this astonishing growth. These are: First, the Southern Pacific Railway, bringing hither not only all the East, but Northern California as well; second, the almost faultless climate of the region; third, the astonishing fertility of the soil; and lastly, the sleepless enterprise of its people. Among these, English-speaking Americans predominate in numbers, wealth, and influence. Next in numbers come the Spanish-speaking Americans, or native Californians, of whom there are in Los Angeles County between ten and twelve thousand. Then follow the representatives of a dozen different languages, among them a scarcity of Frenchmen, but a multiplicity of Chinese and Germans. The Jews are a numerous class, and are said to possess the preponderance of wealth.

The city lies on the west bank of the Los Angeles River, inland from the sea, eighteen miles, on the west, and twenty-one miles on the south. Built chiefly in the valley of that stream, down which it daily urges its way, to the westward and southward, it yet steadily pushes its limits up the hills on the north-west, to-day taking possession of one commanding height, and to-morrow of another. Indeed, the time hastens when all that fine series of elevations lying between the town and the San Fernando Mountains will be crowned with handsome homes, and be laid out in lawns and gardens, where the visitor may delight himself amid an exuberance of trees, flowers, and climbing vines.

Many intelligent persons who have never visited this section of the coast, think of Los Angeles as located immediately upon the ocean shore, just as they suppose Portland, Oregon, to be situated upon the brink of the Columbia River, and should they suddenly be set down in the brisk city, would at once look around for a sight of the big blue sea, or would listen for the roar of its tumbling waves. Nor is this lack of correct geographical knowledge at all surprising. One can not know every thing, and necessarily the maps do not represent the facts accurately. It requires no small fraction of one's time to acquaint himself with the details of matters right at one's door. To grasp all that are embraced within the horizon would demand several "three-score years and ten."

Los Angeles has two outlets to the sea, as follows: Santa Monica, a pretty village lying on the coast, eighteen miles west of the city, was formerly the chief port of landing, but being somewhat ineligible, and San Pedro, on the shore, twenty-one miles south of the city, having been declared by the Government the port of entry for Southern California, the piers were removed from Santa Monica, and the place became simply a sea-side resort and temporary home for such invalids as are benefited by close contact with the ocean. Thus exit from, or entrance to, the metropolis by sea is confined to San Pedro, which, though but an insignificant place, is the entrepôt and outpôt for a large district of Southern California. The point has something of a history, and a short chapter will be devoted to its attractions further on.

If you are not making an ocean trip, but desire simply to breathe the fresh sea air and rest awhile, you may run away either to Santa Monica or to Long Beach. The latter resort lies on the eastern shore of San Pedro Bay. To both points there is railroad communication from the city, and at neither is Old Ocean chary of his tonics. At Santa Monica you have the foaming, roaring surf, breaking in loud thunder on the coast. At Long Beach you may enjoy a carriage ride of several miles on the smooth, hard-packed sand, in addition to the bathing; and should you choose the proper week of the season for your visit, you may have a taste of the literary fare proffered by the "Chautauqua Society of Southern California," which there holds its annual sessions. Excellent accommodations are afforded, if you have forgotten your tent, at both resorts. Long Beach boasts one of the finest hotels in the country.

Not to violate the custom of historians, I suppose I should inform the reader when, and by whom, Los Angeles was founded. Very briefly then: On the 4th of September, 1781, a company of Spanish people—twelve of them men grown—to whom had been granted, at this point on the Los Angeles River, a tract of land six miles square, came upon the ground and laid out this city, giving it the name it bears, and allotting to it the total tract of land. All the original streets traversed this square diagonally. And the stranger must be quick-minded who can to-day determine in which direction he is going without stopping to think. A plaza was laid off and improved, which is even now a central pleasure-ground of the city. Fronting it on the west was erected the parish church. This is still standing, an antique and venerable structure. If I mistake not, one or two more of the first buildings erected by the colony are in existence, but one by one all that class of houses must succumb to the spirit of improvement so rife here.

Nearly due southward through this territory, and east of its middle line, flows the Los Angeles River. Some miles south of the city limits it joins the San Gabriel River, and with it travels to the sea at San Pedro, making a journey of about thirty miles from its source in the Sierra Madre Mountains.

The Los Angeles is one of those streams whose bed, at some points, is above the water. In other words, it flows underground, or is lost in the sand. During the rainy season it enlarges to a broad river, with a powerful current and a dangerous shifting bottom. Widely overflowing its banks, it sweeps away real estate and personal property in a most merciless fashion. Scarcely a season passes in which adventurous men do not lose their lives in attempting to cross it with teams when at its flood. Both driver and horses soon disappear beneath its restless quicksands. But let the early Autumn come! Then the once raging torrent purls along, a narrow, shallow, garrulous brook, which bare-footed children may easily ford.

The rain-fall in Southern California during the Winter of 1884 had not been equaled in twenty-six years. The Los Angeles then rose to a great height. Numberless small tenements, improvidently built too near its brink, were swept from their anchorage and borne away toward the sea, or were ruthlessly wrecked on the spot. From the window of my secure hill-top home I could look down upon the stream and witness its ravages. Several lives were that winter a prey to its waters.

At a point near the city a certain portion of the water of the Los Angeles River is taken up and conveyed hither and thither through seventy-five miles or more of canals, thus forming the Los Angeles Irrigation System. In addition to this, several private water companies supply the fluid, from other sources, to extensive districts, for house, lawn, and garden purposes. The value of effective systems of irrigation to horticulture and vegetable farming in Southern California exceeds all estimate. So rare is frost that a harvest of almost every product which grows here, is nearly an absolute certainty with a moderate supply of water.

The canals are called zangas. The superintendent of the system is styled the zangero. Necessarily he must be a man promptly attentive to business. When the day arrives for a certain orange orchard or vineyard to be flooded, the zangero must have the refreshing liquid ready to laugh and ripple around the roots of the thirsty trees, the moment the gate is opened which admits it to the premises. He must also remember who wants it at night, and see that such parties get it, and in sufficient quantity; nor must he fail to withdraw it from them in the morning.

The soft murmuring of the water as it glides through the zangas in some of the beautiful suburbs of the city is sweet music to the ear, a happy voice sending out joy and gladness. Wherever it is heard are sure to be seen verdure, flowers, and fruit.

One of the comforts a stranger appreciates in Los Angeles is its well-lighted streets. The place can certainly make good its claim to being the best lighted city on the continent. From the central streets to the most outlying alleys the darkness is so far dispelled as to enable the citizens to go about with ease. Electricity is the agent by which the result is accomplished. Mainly the light radiates from a system of tall masts, so located as to in each case illuminate the largest possible area.

In most cities lighted by electricity only the central and wealthier portions enjoy the luxury, the remoter precincts taking the cheaper illuminators. Usually too, in such cities, the high price of property at the heart of things, drives the poor man out into the darkness for a home. In Los Angeles the light has gone out to this class, and may be termed "the poor man's light." Thus, also, are the owners of humble homes, as well as the proprietors of the more elegant ones, reaping the benefit of the augmented value of real estate which the system of lighting helps to create.

A peculiarity of the system is the round, flat "hood," or reflector, which crowns every mast. This both throws the light upon the ground, and prevents its wasteful radiation through the atmosphere.

The area illuminated by this plan is, it is asserted, twenty times greater than the space formerly lighted by gas in the city, while the cost of the arrangement is only about twice that of the latter. Per consequence, the citizens are constantly and generously providing for an extension of the facility. This is soundly politic; a casting of bread upon the waters, which will return a myriad of loaves in *less* than many days.

Three notable ranges of mountains begirt the city of Los Angeles, while farther away, in full view, lie several shorter chains. Within some ten miles of the place, at their nearest point, and stretching off eastward to the San Gorgonio Pass, rise the white summits of the Sierra Madre, bold, rugged elevations, wonderfully suggestive of stability and strength. So near do they appear to-day, in this strangely clear atmosphere, that from my window, when the western sun lights them up, I can plainly see into their riven sides. They are the first object my eye rests upon in the morning, and the last one to be shut out at night. An indescribable solace have they often proved to me, a stranger in this beautiful but melancholy land.

One distinguished summit of the range is Mount

San Bernardino, near the village of that name, and sixty-three miles from Los Angeles. It towers eight thousand five hundred feet above sea-level, and in all dry, clear weather is visible from here. Another lordly projection is Mount Baldy, immediately north of Ontario, and easily accessible from that prosperous colony. Though forty miles from the city, the monarch looks down upon the driving Los Angelans with the air of a watchful deity. North of the city looms up the San Fernando range, shutting out the fertile valley and the once wealthy mission named in honor of that saint. West of us the Santa Monica Mountains sweep proudly down to the verge of the Pacific.

## XII.

## INVALIDS IN SOUTHERN CALIFORNIA.

SUNLIGHT is the life of Southern California at any time, but especially in Winter. With so many snow-capped mountains for near neighbors, and a great sea close at hand to send in, every now and then, vast acres of fog, so dense with moisture as to soon set roofs, door-caps, and window-ledges to dripping musically, Los Angeles would prove but a sorry place for invalids, were it not for an abundance of sunlight, and that of a remarkable quality.

Immediately upon the completion of the Southern Pacific Railway multitudes of ill people flocked to this part of the coast. The accommodations possible for the limited population to offer them, were soon more than exhausted, and not a few sick persons sought ineffectually for entertainment. In the short time which has since elapsed there have been made large additions in the way of hotels and boarding-houses; still each winter the number of invalids has exceeded the added provision for their comfort.

At the present time the city is crowded to its utmost capacity, and hundreds both of invalids and tourists are quartered in the towns adjacent, making the best of the situation. No doubt many of the former class left comfortable homes in the North and East, with mistaken notions of both the climate and the conveniences of life here. Few realized that, notwithstanding Southern California was more than a century ago in the hands of the Spaniards, it is a comparatively new land, and among improvements to come, are facilities for the proper care of a large force of diseased and disabled men and women. Particularly true is this of all the new and smaller villages. Nowhere are there ample hospital accommodations. Hotel room is inadequate. Indeed, many things are but at the starting point. It deserves to be said, however, that the readiness of the citizens to serve, and even faithfully nurse, invalid strangers, is something remarkable, and often far exceeds just demands. A more hospitable, large-hearted, and sympathetic people does not exist than are the American residents of Southern California. To this fact the writer can bear grateful testimony.

Recently an officer of the Young Men's Christian Association, who, more than any one else, perhaps, is aware of the disappointments encountered by many who come to the coast for health, said to the writer:

"Emphasis should undoubtedly be laid by parties writing back to the States, upon the fact that within a very short time Los Angeles has leaped from a quiescent old Spanish town into a rapidly growing American city, but that as yet its limits and provisions are insufficient for the complete accommodation of the thousands of tourists and invalids who converge here from all parts of the continent. The city is simply taxed beyond its capacity, and in spite of the excellent intentions of the citizens, some sick strangers fare hardly.

"And another thing: Frequently women have accompanied husbands to this coast who were just on the verge of death, and have suddenly been left here without means for returning to their families. For such the city has no proper refuge until they can either find employment or receive help from their friends. In several instances the philanthropic citizens have promptly contributed means for returning them to their relatives."

These statements were made in 1884. Since then the deficiencies have to a considerable extent been met. Large hotels and boarding-houses have multiplied all over the region. Nevertheless, in the Winter of 1886, so vast was the influx of visitors from every quarter that shelter could barely be found for them all. In the city of Los Angeles, at present, as will appear toward the close of this work, are in progress active measures for erecting a spacious home for such women as may at any time be left here in the pitiable plight above mentioned. And a year hence, probably, abundant hospital attentions can be guaranteed all those who will require such ministries.

Consumptives and sufferers from rheumatism usually picture to themselves an entire winter here out of doors, in the enjoyment of genial sunshine, and free from annoyance by cruel frost or piercing wind. But the Winters are not uniform. During that of 1884, for instance, those invalids who survived the change of climate, which is very great and puts to an immense strain most persons far advanced in disease, found themselves confined to their rooms nearly one-half the time, and every day in need of fire, especially if they were located on the sunless side of their residences. Added to this, some missed the gentle ministries which so much conduced to their pleasure at home. Others failed, it may be, to obtain the dishes which tempted appetite and kept up strength. Under such circumstances, those unattended by friends felt particularly desolate. Their maladies rather increased than relaxed, perhaps. Happily those who had the means could return to their homes, if sufficient vitality remained to endure the long journey. But what could those do who possessed but slender purses, or had no helpful friends? They could do but one thing: abide where they were until they entered upon their final rest. That has been the sad fate of many. Then a few Christian men and women, or a half-dozen members of some benevolent order to which they have belonged, will sorrowfully consign them to the arms of Mother Earth.

These are strong and not very cheerful statements. Yet are they true, and scarcely less so to-day than they were three years ago. One needs but to note the number of funerals held at the undertaking establishments, or to observe the array of newly made graves in the cemeteries, to be convinced on this point. Most of the graves in which sleep the once lonely and needy, will be found marked with but a narrow board, and upon it inscribed the occupants' name, age, and the date of his death.

A resident of the city has several times remarked to me: "Should we attend the funerals of all the invalid strangers who die here we should do little else." Some two weeks ago a member of one of the well-known transcontinental excursion firms stated that of five young men, victims of consumption, who came to the coast with his last company, three passed away within a week after their arrival. Not far from our door there entered into rest the other day a noble young woman, a teacher in the schools of Canada. She had not a relative this side the Dominion. Hope of regaining health induced her to undertake the long, wearying journey alone. The draught upon her strength was too great. Typhoid fever came in and ended the scene. Leaving means too scanty to convey her remains to her home, humane hands consigned them to the grave here.

What, then, shall the great army of sufferers in our colder latitudes do? Not come to California? Very decidedly, no; not after death is at the door. But come when your disease begins to develop. Make the sacrifice of leaving friends and business earlier. Study the climate of different localities on or near the coast. Or, what is better, have your physician do it for you, and before you leave home. By all means, get into the right place for *your* malady. Remember that sunlight in Southern California is as necessary to the life of sick persons as it is to the life of vegetation. Hence secure rooms, if possible, which the sunlight enters at least a part of the day; if all day, the better for you. Understand, however, that not even this potent agency can restore to health persons just ready to die upon their arrival here.

Conversing with a leading physician of the city on this subject to-day, he expressed substantially the following opinions, which, though a partial repetition of what has already been said, I think best to insert here:

In cases of consumption, where the disease is not so far developed as to make recovery impossible anywhere, it is a good thing to come to Southern California, for three reasons. First—A change of climate and locality is secured. Other things being equal, this is an advantage. Second—There being, *usually,* little rain-fall, and no frost to be considered, especially on the hills, opportunity is offered to live much out of doors; and life in the air and sunlight is the consumptive's prime requirement. Third—Once here, choice can easily be made between the moist, salt air of the sea, the dry, bracing atmosphere of the foot-hills, the vigorous breath of the open cañons, and the genial air of the broad, sunny plains or verdant valleys. It has been learned that the climate of no single situation affects all consumptives alike. One will improve on the border of the sea, its stiff breeze and chilling fog helping. From these the next patient must run for his life. Another will take in mouthfuls of health with every breath on a hill-top. The reasons for this are very apparent. In the various patients the disease is at all stages of progress. Then each sufferer's ailment is due to a different cause. All these are matters which should be intelligently studied.

A prudent course, perhaps, is to make Los Angeles your initial point. From there removal to other localities can be effected at small cost of time, money, and strength. The city lies with an hour's ride of the two sea-side resorts already named. And decking, like lovely gems, the great plain which skirts the base of the Sierra Madre Mountains, from the charming village of Pasadena, eastward seventy miles or more, are the pretty towns of Garvanza, Monrovia, San Gabriel, Pomona, Ontario, Etiwanda, and San Bernardino, all offering special inducements in the way of scenery, situation, climate, good water, or healing springs. All lie near or upon the Southern Pacific Railway, and afford one or more well-kept hotels, while many of the private families open their homes to strangers in cases of exigency. San Bernardino treats rheumatic people to mud baths. Ontario tents asthmatic visitors in the mouth of her San Antonio cañon. Consumptives may distribute themselves all over the prairie, as suits their case. Santa Ana, farther south on the plain, is said to be an excellent point for them. In some of these places there is not so remarkable a difference between the air of the day and the night, as at Los Angeles.

San Diego, on the coast, one hundred and thirty miles south of Los Angeles, and connected therewith by rail and by steamer, undoubtedly offers better conditions for the cure of consumption and throat disorders than does this city. But once more patients diagree. A clergyman from the vicinity of Boston, who had for several months tested the climate of San Diego for a severe throat affection, said he "could breathe most freely where fogs are frequent." On the contrary, a friend in this city, similarly afflicted, finds respiration most difficult in a moist atmosphere, and therefore chose as her place of residence a delightful hill-top above the altitude of ordinary fogs.

## XIII.

## WHAT SHALL WE WEAR?

THE question of clothing on the Pacific Coast is an important one. Ordinarily the same apparel may be worn the year round, and should be composed of such garments as form the indoor Winter raiment throughout the East. Neither old nor young, sick nor well, should stray hither unsupplied with both light and heavy wraps. Of nights and mornings they are indispensable to comfort, especially on days when the sun refuses to shine. Happily such days are few. As has been said, from the sun, in large part, come the cheer, the enjoyment, the recuperation, and strength so ardently anticipated by the thousands who seek the coast in Winter. From the first of October until the middle of June, warm shawls, Newmarkets, fur-lined cloaks, and heavy overcoats are in brisk demand, except, perhaps, at midday, and are often welcome at evening throughout the Summer. Light clothing, made of linen, cambrics, and similar fabrics, is never needed except on a few days in Midsummer, and even then can be easily dispensed with.

Last October there came to Los Angeles a lady from—somewhere in the East—bringing an ample Summer wardrobe, and leaving at home most of her Winter attire. She expected to find the temperature ranging in the neighborhood of ninety or one hundred degrees. Late in April that portion of her outfit remained snugly packed in her trunks. As she went up the coast early in May, passed the Summer in San Francisco, where such apparel seldom gets an airing, made an Autumn visit in Oregon, and returned to her home in December, her thin dresses had a long, restful trip.

A bright woman at my side says:

"When I left Michigan, a few years ago, a doleful asthmatic, with scarcely a hope of relief, even in Southern California, my friends laughed at the idea of my bringing flannels. 'What possible need of such garments,' they asked, 'in a land of perpetual bloom?' So I left my warm underwear to freeze in the Wolverine State, while I did the same thing in Los Angeles."

There is another point: Many invalids delay their journey to the Pacific Coast until too late in the season, numbers coming towards the middle of Winter. The danger of taking cold is then much increased, since heavy rains are imminent. Pneumonia comes with them, and is on the alert for strangers with weak lungs, often quickly changing the scene for the sufferers, by shutting out this world. It is stated that about ninety of every one hundred persons contract a severe cold immediately upon reaching the coast. This is a sort of toll the climate exacts for the delights it means to confer afterwards. A little caution exercised for some days might cheat it out of that revenue. Dress warmly; avoid draughts of air; carry a wrap on your arm, if you go out at midday to remain after four o'clock.

Upon arriving in Los Angeles health-seekers should avoid, particularly in Winter, apartments on the first floors of brick, adobe, and even frame dwellings, if the floors are laid near the ground. An adobe house is seldom more than one story in height. The floors are rarely raised above the soil; hence the rains render them damp and unwholesome. Moreover, the initiated claim that the older adobe residences are little better than hot-beds for engendering malaria. Malignant fevers lurk among their sand and gravel. In all such quarters fire is the more indispensable, and in

Southern California the word fire means something. A large portion of the coal used comes from Australia, and each ton costs a small fortune. The crooked roots of the "grease-bush," together with the trimmings from the eucalyptus, pepper, and other trees, constitute the staple for wood. Coal-oil is meeting with some favor here as a fuel, but the heat from it is not the most agreeable in living rooms for the seriously ill.

## XIV.

## A FORMER HOME OF GENERAL AND MRS. HANCOCK.

A CURIOSITY which finds satisfaction in visiting localities where flagrant crimes have been committed, is a quality utterly lacking in the writer. I would not walk one rod to see where a notorious criminal had lived or died. Nor would I write one line to spread the fame or perpetuate the name of such a being. But I freely confess that I find pleasure in looking upon the dwelling-place, in contemplating the work, in standing beside the grave of man or woman who has spent this life in well-doing. In such places, in such work, there is inspiration. Something about them always suggests the character of the persons, their loveliness, genuineness, taste, and power, and strengthens you.

These notions found a practical application this morning in a visit paid to the former home of General—then Captain—and Mrs. W. S. Hancock, who for several years before the Rebellion were residents of Los Angeles. Descending the long, zigzag, public staircase which leads from upper to lower Third

Street, and thence passing on down to Main Street, and crossing that diagonally, turning a little to the right, I stood in front of a square brick cottage, one story in height, and painted red. A wide veranda, ample for a half dozen persons to sit and chat at eventide, shaded its two front doors. This spot afforded a view of the magnificent sunsets, and from all I have learned was the favorite resort of the few American residents of Los Angeles in that early day.

The house was built for Captain Hancock about the year 1859, by the present mayor of the city, Mr. E. C. Thom, himself a devoted personal friend of the Hancocks. The dwelling is a duplicate of the one in which Mr. Thom then resided, and which now stands on the adjoining lot, to the left of the cottage, the mayor's present stately home being on the right of it, with a narrow street intervening. In the yard surrounding the cottage, their trunks half buried in a mound of loose earth, stand several orange-trees, now destitute of fruit. Originally this yard, set with flowers, vines, fruit, and ornamental trees, formed a scene of beauty which both families enjoyed. Mrs. Hancock is said to have been passionately fond of flowers.

Hearing the sounds of workmen inside, and both

front doors standing wide open, I walked in, and in one of the back rooms found a young man, who, upon learning my errand, very courteously acted the part of host to the empty house and furnished me the information I sought. The plan of the dwelling is very peculiar, and suggests that it was devised for both the pleasure and the convenient entertainment of guests, and back of that, that the builder himself was a man hospitably inclined. The main part is done off into four square rooms, each opening into two others, around a square post in the center. Both front rooms have a street entrance, three large windows, a fire-place—not grate—with marble mantel, and two doors opening into the succeeding apartment. These rear rooms once opened into additions, ells, or wings, which served the purpose of kitchen, laundry, and servants' quarters, and partly inclosed the presidio between them. These wings are now removed, and in the thick walls of the main building appear large apertures, in which are inserted heavy screws, ready for transferring the whole structure to the rear of the lot, where it will serve as shops, the ground it now occupies being required for a new street opening between it and the residence of the mayor. Thus will be banished to partial obscurity and to business purposes a tenement which was once the happy home of Almira Russell Hancock, then, as now, one of the noblest and most beautiful of American women.

In the society of this frontier post Mrs. Hancock seems to have shone conspicuously, not for her personal beauty only, but for her rare charms of mind, grace of manners, and kindness of heart. The sweetness of her disposition forms a subject of remark among old acquaintances here to-day. Men and women alike, who knew her well in the various relations of life, speak of her with admiration, uttering never a word of criticism. A gentlemen prominent here in that day, said, speaking of her this morning:

"I have never known a woman like her. She was obliging to an extreme. Accomplished in music, and though herself an Episcopalian, she long played the organ in our mingled Protestant services, with as much zeal and interest as though she were a member of all the churches represented."

Another, for thirty years a personal friend and correspondent of General Hancock, said, with the feeling a brother might manifest:

"I hesitate to speak of her as she deserves, for I know her dislike of publicity, her aversion to display. But it is true that she seemed to possess every trait that can adorn the character of woman. During her life in Los Angeles, she was, to a remarkable degree, cheerful, hopeful, thoughtful of the poor, pitiful towards the sorrowing, and always ready to do any thing that would conduce to the general welfare of the community. She was a wise mother, and reared her two children, Ada and Russell Hancock, with the future of their lives always in view. She shone in society, but more brightly at home. Added to all this, she was beautiful to look at, and had the most expressive eyes I ever saw."

"The years which have intervened," he continued, "between their departure from this city, in 1861, I think, when the general was ordered to the east, at the outbreak of the Rebellion, and their recent visit here, while they have greatly elevated her in social position, appear only to have mellowed the qualities we admired, not destroyed them."

"There were so few of us, American residents, in Los Angeles then," said another, who, possessing, like Mrs. Hancock, an obliging and helpful spirit, had acted as chorister at the much prized Protestant services, "that we used to count heads every Sunday. Often there were only thirty of us all told."

"The daughter was a lovely girl," said the first speaker. "Though she was young when they left here, she was very attractive. Her death occurred in New York, some eight or nine years since, I can not tell just how long. She was eighteen years of age, had just graduated from some school in that vicinity, and was considered much accomplished. To her parents it was a terrible bereavement.

"Russell, the son is now a successful planter at Clarksdale, Mississippi. He must be about thirty years of age. He is a mechanical genius, and constructs almost every kind of machinery which the exigencies of his business require. Neither of the children were born in Los Angeles. Captain Hancock was transferred to this post, then the principal military station of Southern California, from Fort Tejon, in Kern County."

The "recent visit" of General and Mrs. Hancock to Los Angeles, mentioned by this friend, occurred the first week of January, 1884, and was a time for general rejoicing on the part of those who had known and loved them far back in the fifties. A royal welcome was given them. There was an enthusiastic procession of the citizens in their honor on New Year's Day, and, if I mistake not, a banquet was tendered them in the evening.

When it was known that Los Angeles would be included in General Hancock's western trip, the mayor of the city requested the work of demolishing their cottage to cease until after their departure, in order that Mrs. Hancock might see her early home as nearly in the state she left it as possible. After seeing it the excellent woman remarked that she had "spent the happiest hours of her life in that little brick cottage."

Mrs. Anna Ozier, the widow of Judge Isaac S. R. Ozier, who was judge of the Federal Court for Southern California in 1854, was one of the first five American women who settled in Los Angeles after the accession of California, and was an intimate friend of Mrs. Hancock. She still resides in this city, and entertained her old friends when they were here. In a talk with her, after I had visited the dismantled cottage, she cited this reminiscence of them, among many others. I give her words:

"One day during a season of heavy rainfall, like that we have had this Winter, the entire north wall of the captain's house fell out, flat upon the ground. The soil of Los Angeles has a migratory disposition, and a few days' heavy rain are enough to start it traveling in all directions. Besides, the brick we got here, in those days, were very porous, and they, too, filling with water, were disposed to change quarters.

"It was no trifling occurrence, but the captain and Mrs. Hancock took the trouble with the greatest good nature. Happening to be coming up the street that evening about tea-time, I saw the family sitting at table as happy as if nothing were the matter.

"Did I know them intimately? Mercy, yes! They lived near us three years, and there was hardly an evening when we were not together. Mrs. Hancock had the pleasantest disposition of any woman I ever knew, and a brother could not have been kinder to me, through all these years, than has been General Hancock."

"If republics are ungrateful, you are not, I see."

"No; and I shall never forgive this nation for not making General Hancock President."

## XV.

## CALIFORNIA'S GREAT HISTORIAN.

SOMETIME in the latter part of March, 1884, I received from the wife of Mr. Hubert H. Bancroft, author of the "History of the Pacific Coast States," a note stating that her husband, herself, and family would visit Los Angeles at an early date in April, and while there would "be glad to see me." The lady and her children had wintered, I believe, in the Ojai Valley, and now, with the advent of Spring, were exchanging that "most healthful of all valleys on the globe" for the sea breeze at San Diego, two hundred and twenty miles farther south. I had sought from Mrs. Bancroft, as she was within quick reach, certain information pertaining to her husband's great work; hence her kindly reply.

Accordingly, next day after their arrival I called at the Kimball Mansion, situated on New High Street, where I found them comfortably quartered, with their family of four children, all under eight years of age. During the informal interview

I had opportunity to note how delightful is the home atmosphere which surrounds Mr. Bancroft, and also to learn many interesting facts connected with his early life, and with the founding of his unique historical library in San Francisco. Most persons take pleasure in reading sketches of the life and labors of such men as Mr. Bancroft. I therefore present a hastily drawn picture of the great historian and his family before speaking of his unexampled literary undertaking.

Mrs. Bancroft is an attractive and cultured woman, whose married life covers nine years. She is very youthful in appearance, has a slight figure, blue eyes, light hair, and a fair complexion. Her manner is extremely cordial, making one forget that she was the acquaintance of but an hour, instead of a life-time. She is pleased with her husband's growing reputation as an author, has a keen appreciation of the importance of his work, and so far as she has the power, compels affairs to bend to its accomplishment.

The two eldest children are magnificent specimens of boyhood; strong, athletic little fellows, with massive heads on their shoulders, and within their breasts a mighty purpose to get out of every hour of time the utmost of boy enjoyment. And if I judged correctly, their parents mean this purpose shall be accomplished, but within limits which shall not infringe upon the rights of others, nor destroy the capacity of their children to enjoy the higher pleasures of life by and by. From some things which Mr. Bancroft has written, I conclude that a favorite opinion of his, is, that in the not very distant future the—let us say American—race will have made so great advancement in what is termed "sublime culture," as to materially lessen the moral distance between God and this nation. And, very possibly, the man's hope is, that his sons may live and be fitted to take part in the affairs of that auspicious time. Just where fifty years more of material and national development, like that of the past half century—were our rapid progress in countless enormous iniquities to suddenly cease—would bring us, even the seer endowed with keenest vision could hardly foretell. Should it be at dawn of an era so blessed, any expectations of that nature which the distinguished historian may entertain, might possibly be realized. For, judging from his mode of managing his lively sons, he is just the man to train them for a life under such conditions, and thus do his part towards ushering in the glorious day he paints.

In the fair daughter, younger than her brothers,

scarcely less interest centers. I saw her but a few moments, but they were enough to convince me that, while her brothers are small bundles of condensed action, she is a little package of tranquillity, just the article needed in the other end of the balance. The fourth child is a son, about three years old at the present date.

Hubert How Bancroft is a native of Ohio, and adds another name to her list of eminent men. Next to California, that State should feel honored in him, and take interest in his great work. He was born in Granville, May 5, 1832, and is now fifty-five years of age. Mr. Bancroft is a person of medium height, rather heavy set, broad chested, with square shoulders, which incline forward slightly, the result, no doubt, of years of work with the pen. He has a large head, thick, iron-gray hair, dark eyes, and a Southern complexion. His manner is frank and kindly. He impresses a stranger as a man of honest purpose, and great decision of character. The sum of his school education was obtained in the district schools of Ohio before he was sixteen years of age.

At that period Mr. Bancroft left home, going to Buffalo, where he was employed in a book-store owned by his brother-in-law, Mr. George H. Derby,

Here, for some reason, he failed of the advantage he anticipated, and closed his engagement at the end of a year. A portion of his journey to Buffalo was made on the Ohio Canal. Being rich, not in this world's goods, but in having an uncle who was the captain of a boat on that ancient water-way, he proposed to ride one of the horses attached thereto to the city of Cleveland, in payment for his fare. His uncle accepted the offer, and the future historian rode into the beautiful Forest City in the capacity of a canal-boy. Mr. Bancroft mentioned this circumstance as an amusing experience of his youth, rather than otherwise. I wondered at the moment if, in relating it, he thought at all of the second martyr President, the beginning of whose path to eminence also ran along the brink of that canal.

Leaving Buffalo Mr. Bancroft laid his course for the Pacific Coast, *via* Cape Horn, being intrusted by Mr. Derby with an invoice of books and stationery with which to open the book-trade in the city of San Francisco. Months were consumed in making the passage, and before he reached the Golden Gate Mr. Derby had died; and upon his landing an order met him to re-ship the goods to Buffalo. He, however, made a fortunate sale of them instead, and remitted the proceeds to Mrs.

Derby, thereby much improving her financial condition.

As early as 1856 Mr. Bancroft had not only become known on the coast for his habits of industry and economy, but had accumulated means to found a book-store of his own in San Francisco. Twenty-five years later the establishment was one of the first of its kind in the world. About this time his grand history project began to take serious shape in his mind. Repeatedly during his residence on the coast, had his attention been drawn to the fact that important material for a true history of California was daily losing beyond recovery. He resolved to take steps to preserve it. Immediately he began to collect books, pamphlets, letters, and documents, pertaining thereto. By degrees the field of these labors widened, until it embraced the entire western half of the continent, from the Rocky Mountains to the great ocean; from Alaska to Panama, including Central America and Mexico.

In pursuance of his purpose now, he not only visited the eastern part of the Continent, but made several journeys to Europe, each trip adding priceless material to his collection. During 1868, with twelve thousand volumes of these treasures on hand, gathered at an immense cost, he conceived the idea of giving them to the world in the form of one continuous, carefully written history. But the question was: Could he accomplish such a feat? The task involved an unflinching purpose, years of unremitting toil, the outlay of a fortune, and the possession of fine literary ability. Did he possess that? was another question. Undismayed by this dread presentation of the case, he determined to undertake the prodigious work.

Accordingly, releasing himself from the burden of business in his book-store, he installed his brother, Mr. A. L. Bancroft, manager-in chief of the establishment; and, engaging a score of assistants, began arranging his material in the fourth story of their building. His first step was to carefully index the vast collection, just as an author would index the subjects in his book. Thus his task was at once greatly facilitated. This work occupied an average of six persons ten years, and cost upwards of eighty thousand dollars.

Meanwhile another set of scribes, taking these indexes, abstracted from them the information desired in reference to any given part of the Territory. This was known as the "rough material." Next, a third class of writers, better qualified, elaborated this matter into proper historical form, and submitted the result to Mr. Bancroft, who carefully revised the work, rewriting such portions as he chose. Sometimes, however, beginning back with the indexes, he himself wrote out important portions entirely.

During all this time the collection of books, letters, newspapers, maps of the coast, and of the country, and annals in manuscript, went on, until over thirty thousand volumes were accumulated, the whole constituting a library unapproachable as to value in this country, particularly to writers on special historical themes, and it related to an area equal to one-twelfth of the earth's surface.

In addition to this, his deputies had long been busy, all over this territory, taking notes from aged pioneers, military men, statesmen, and surviving members of old Spanish families, all of whom, with the antecedent Indian tribes, had helped make its history. The result of this movement was thousands of manuscripts filled with the deeds or reminiscences of as many living people, all of it absosutely original, and nowhere else existing.

At the same time another force was busy copying papers in county, state, and national archives. Nor was this all. Interested persons all over the land contributed piles of original documents, swelling the mass to vast proportions. Finally this material was bound in many folio volumes, inestimable in value as sources of reference.

Twenty-five years in all had now been devoted to this work of aggregation. But in an hour fire might reduce the treasure to ashes. To save it from such a fate, Mr. Bancroft determined to place over it a shelter absolutely fire-proof. The time had been brought down to 1881. Accordingly, during that year he erected, far out on Valencia Street in San Francisco, a large, two-story, fire-proof repository, and therein, in orderly arrangement, set up his possessions. This building with its contents forms the famous Bancroft Library, report of which has gone so far abroad.

All this was the munificent preparation for what the papers have termed Mr. Bancroft's "stupendous undertaking," namely, the writing the "History of the Pacific Coast States of North America." But introductory to this, and according to a plan which shows Mr. Bancroft's correct judgment, as regards the order in which the different epochs of American history should be presented, was to be published, a "History of the *Native Races* of the Pacific Coast States," in five volumes. One of these was to deal with the wild tribes of the entire region, and another with the "Civilized Nations of Mexico and Central America." These five volumes are already issued. After them comes the history proper, covering the extent of country I have designated, and embraced in thirty volumes.

Closely related to the history, but more effective, published apart from it, come four volumes, entitled, first, "California Pastoral," being an account of life and times under the early Catholic missionaries; second, "California Inter Pocula," or life during the gold mining period; and third, "Popular Tribunals," or the acts of California Vigilance Committees. Thus the complete great work includes thirty-nine volumes, and is a vast repository, packed from cover to cover with facts pertaining to the habits, customs, sorrows, pleasures, religions, and achievements of the races which have successively held sway on the Pacific Coast. Mr. Bancroft expects the year 1890 to witness the completion of his task, should he live to urge forward its composition and publication.

Mr. Bancroft's work will live after him. As well might we relegate to the periods which produced them the histories of Rollin, D'Aubigné, Macaulay, and Prescott, as to confine this gigantic record of past deeds and events to the present.

No, we must accord it life for all time. There will be, however, this difference in its usefulness. The above authors are read by thousands upon thousands of the common people, because in scope, and time, and subject they are limited to narrow bounds, and cost but a trifle. But from its very size and expense the "History of the Pacific States of North America" will find entrance only into public libraries and the book-cases of the rich.

Notwithstanding, there is in the work much of interest for readers old and young. What boy or girl in all the Union would not sit entranced over the volume on the wild tribes of the coast? In some parts its style is plain even to homeliness, but it is suited to the subject, and allows the interest to flag not for a moment. In other portions the story runs on in clear, ringing, picturesque sentences. Savage men and women stand before the reader, creatures of a wonderfully distinct photography. One lives among them; sees with his own eyes their homes, children, old people; goes with them to weddings, funerals, and wars; is interested, amused, or shocked, according to the circumstances. Take, for instance, the description of the *temescal*, or sweat-house, an institution common to many of the tribes. Virtually one enters the strange place, feels the effects of the heat and steam, enjoys the final drowsiness and comfort, and upon emerging from the pit wonders not at all that the vagabonds of the tribes are often the victims of some pain or disease which can be driven out of them only by a thorough steaming and a long, sound sleep; nor that in the Winter these ills are most frequent.

The second volume, treating of the civilized races of Mexico and Central America, is a narrative of marvelous life and doings. Its pages are equally captivating for the cultured or untutored reader. There Spain found and destroyed "a civilization in some respects greater than her own." There she caused rivers of innocent human blood to flow, in the name of religion and for love of gold. In these two volumes are depicted every phase of human nature, from the reptile-eating cave-dwellers to the enlightened Maya-Quicha people of the southern table-lands. To the last line their history is a tale which holds spell-bound the one who believes that "every thing connected with man deserves man's most careful study."

Mr. Bancroft's account of the Spanish conquest of Peru is the most clear and succinct I have ever read. One finishes the chapters with a well-defined idea of the cause and the manner of the Incarial overthrow. Sketched to the life are the mercenary men who conceived and accomplished it. Their motives, their insatiable greed, their disregard of human life, are brought out into noonday light. A mere handful of starved, insubordinate, and desperate adventurers, they conquer, when at the zenith of its glory, an empire, opulent and teeming with people, and so re-enact the rôle of Hernando Cortez in the subjugation of Mexico.

For specialists in the many fields of literature, this unequaled history will prove a mine of wealth for all the future of America. Scarcely a question can arise, touching the race, but here may find something to the point.

## XVI.

## An Ill Wind That Blew Good.

THE six weeks rain-fall which drenched the soil of Southern California during February and March of this year, 1884, will long be remembered for the freshets it produced, the lives it cost, and the property it destroyed. On several of the streams between this city and the desert, the bridges of the Southern Pacific road were either swept away or rendered unsafe, detaining passengers and mails for days in succession, at points where supplies were difficult to obtain. Buildings and stock were caught up by the resistless currents, wrecking the former and drowning the latter. Acres of land were spirited away to the ocean. Many kinds of business were seriously checked. Invoices of Spring goods dallied on the desert. Nearly every body looked doleful and felt apprehensive. The local weather prophets enhanced the trouble by foretelling still heavier floods before affairs should mend. Invalids, scattered in all directions, confined indoors most of the time, sighed for the latitudes where frost imprisons the streams and adorns the window-panes.

But after awhile the wind which had so long blown ill changed its course, and as generously blew good. The earth, hard as stone, and almost impossible to cultivate when dry, had been wet down to an unusual depth, and could now be worked to advantage. This gave a fresh impetus to tree-planting all over the broad plain stretching between the Sierra Madre and the sea, south and east of the city. The citizens of Santa Ana, Orange, Tustin, Westminster, and other thriving villages dotting this plain, awoke to the value of the opportunity, and early in April were setting trees. Meeting a tourist from that section of the country this morning, I inquired what varieties of trees were planted in largest numbers.

"The orange, lemon, lime, olive, apricot, pear, and others, for fruit; the pepper and eucalyptus, for shade and ornament," he replied. "The nurserymen," he continued, "are paying the owners of teams ten dollars per day for drawing trees to purchasers. On my way up to the city I rode some distance with one of these teamsters, who had on his wagon ten thousand apricot, pear, and olive trees for horticulturists at some point. He said he distributed nearly that number daily. And how they take hold and grow! Hardly is the ground well packed around the roots ere they show themselves at home in the new situation."

In one's rambles on this plain, one hears not a little about the change of climate likely to result from this lavish extension of orchards, groves, and vineyards. There are those who think the movement will, in time, materially shorten the long summer drought of past days by bringing down showers of rain. Every tree, it is contended, set in the valleys or on the hill-sides becomes a leafy reservoir for the storage of water. Not only so, it performs a double duty in the case. The roots retain the water which otherwise would flow away, especially in sloping situations; while the top, a manifold canopy sheltering the ground, prevents its evaporation from about the roots. At the same time the leaves, from their million mouths, pour into the air, of a sunny day, an invisible cloud of moisture. With millions of trees united in the beautiful work, the atmosphere will be charged with vapor, which, condensing in the night, or by coming in contact with a body of cooler air, will descend in showers, blessing the earth.

Possibly the thousands of acres of trees already well-grown on this vast prairie, where once scarce a tree was to be seen, may account for the several copious showers which fell in the Summer of that year. But whether tree-planting shall or shall not greatly affect the climate in Los Angeles and San Diego counties, the work is certain to produce business, fill the local markets with luscious fruits, and render very picturesque the country. Therefore may the desirable industry flourish.

If the reader will glance at a well-executed map of these counties, he will find a branch of the Southern Pacific Railway extending from Los Angeles south-eastwardly to the bright little village of Santa Ana, at present the terminus of the road. The distance is forty-two miles. The route lies through the rich plain of which we have been speaking, and which was once a part of the celebrated San Joaquin rancho. It is one of the most productive portions of semi-tropic California. Besides the towns I have already mentioned, those of Downey, Norwalk, and Anaheim, with their extensive orchards and vineyards, grace leagues of country along the way. From the window of my room on this hill-top I can trace the location of some of these places, as I look down the Los Angeles Valley toward the sea. Since this is a bright morning, suppose we step aboard the cars, take a run through the fine district, and spend the night at Santa Ana.

As we speed along you notice that all manner of fruits are cultivated—oranges, lemons, olives, apricots, apples, grapes, figs, bananas, English walnuts, and many others.

## DOWNEY.

At Downey, named for a recent governor of California, and twelve miles out, we come to a community of several hundred inhabitants. The place is noted for the cultivation of figs and grapes. At an exhibit of county fruits, held in Los Angeles in October, my attention was drawn to a magnificent display of Malaga grapes from here. The weight of nearly every cluster approximated to four pounds. Beside these, its roots firmly imbedded in a tub of sand, was stationed a vigorous Malaga vine, weighed down with enormous bunches. How the slender branches could sustain such a burden through the season of growth was a wonder. Close at hand lay small heaps of nine other varieties, very tempting to sight and taste, among them the Muscat, Sultana, Sweetwater, and Flaming Tokay.

But of greater interest to me than these was an array of large, rich figs, fresh from the trees, four varieties, the White Smyrna, Brown Turkish, Plymouth Rock—chickens, by no means—and the New

Pacific, a fig remarkable for its fine flavor and quick-drying quality. The White Smyrna having been longest known has the widest reputation and readiest market. The New Pacific seriously threatens to supersede it, however. Fresh, ripe figs bear lengthy transportation no better than do ripe peaches; and picked before they are fully ripe, are not a particle more savory than are green tomatoes.

Under a California sun, not too hot, figs dry in from three to four days. For domestic use, housekeepers often cure them in the oven of the cooking-stove or range. Care must always be taken, of course, to preserve the proper temperature, or they will sour. The fig produces the second year from planting, and bears at the same time both green and ripe fruit. Set in damp situations the tree thrives like the willow; in dry positions it requires irrigation. There are orchards numbering twenty-five hundred trees, in full bearing, at Downey. Fresh figs are very cheap in Los Angeles, but the dried fruit retails at twenty-five cents the pound. Countless private gardens in Southern California contain one or more fig trees of a good variety.

Before continuing our journey I wish to call attention to a gentleman who makes a specialty of raising bananas on the foot-hills, some three miles or so from Los Angeles. This is Mr. J. W. Potts, to whom the city newspapers, during the great flood of last Winter, gave the euphonious sobriquet of "Prophet Potts." In size and general appearance Mr. Potts closely resembles the picture of old Father Time in the ancient Webster spelling-book. He has a short, slight figure, iron-gray hair, a small face, a sharp chin, and an exceedingly attenuated voice. He speaks rapidly and nervously. His manner partakes of the searching investigative kind. Equipped with hour-glass and scythe he would readily be mistaken for the original of the spelling-book illustration.

Mr. Potts came to Los Angeles from somewhere in the East, in the ever-memorable year of 1849, an enthusiast, not in gold-hunting, but in fruit-culture, as he himself told me. Having long been a close observer of the laws which operate in the domain of the atmosphere, he some time before it occurred, predicted the very unusual rain-fall of last Winter, adding that it would be attended with disaster and heavy loss. The fulfillment of the prediction secured him his title.

For four years past Mr. Potts has paid considerable attention to raising bananas on his farm among the foot-hills. He asserts that of his three hundred and fifty trees, from twelve to fourteen feet in height, not one has ever been touched by frost. During the year 1883 these trees were laden with the delicious fruit at every stage of growth, and requiring some nine months for its perfection. Some of this fruit hung on the trees unharmed during the Winter of 1883–84, one of the most trying, for cold, ever known here. This is regarded as conclusive evidence of the safety of tender fruits growing on elevated situations near Los Angeles. Mr. Potts irrigates a portion of his trees once during the season, and others not at all. Their position decides the question, I suppose. This gentleman says he was present, over thirty years ago, when Mr. William Wolfskill planted his famous orange orchard, a spot which few visitors to Los Angeles fail to see, and avers that not once since then has there been frost sufficient in Southern California to injure large orange trees.

### ANAHEIM.

Two things give Anaheim, our next point on the road, prominence in the country and the newspapers. These are its wineries and ostrich farm. The rearing of ostriches being a rare undertaking in America, these birds excite much curiosity on the part of visitors to the Pacific Coast. The ostriches are farmed about seven miles from the village, and at present number forty or more. I have not seen them, but have been told that about half of them are full grown, and measure, from the ground to the top of the back, from eight to nine feet. The ostrich is a timid fowl, but the males when irritated are disposed to be violent, towards their mates, and towards men and animals. It is reported that even their former careful and humane superintendent, Dr. Sketchley, occasionally became the object of their wrath at Anaheim; and, also, that one of the birds, a Hercules for strength, becoming enraged at his mate not long ago, raised one of his powerful legs and dealt her a terrific blow, when quickly she was no more. I will not vouch for the truth of these statements. Undoubtedly the African bird holds, as many men do, that he has a right to strike his wife. Dr. Sketchley, no longer at Anaheim, but now actively engaged in founding a zoological garden, on a scale of munificence in keeping with every thing Californian, a few miles north-west of Los Angeles, among the foot-hills of the San Fernando Mountains, can answer for himself as to the treatment he received from his Anaheim wards. Here also he is planting a colony of these birds of elegant plumage.

Like the eucalyptus and the pepper tree, the ostrich loses its attractiveness as age creeps on. Hence the juvenile members of the Anaheim family are most in favor with visitors. Some of them are now about the size of full-grown turkeys, and are prospectively very valuable on account of their feathers. The first plucking takes place when the bird is about a year and a half old.

The eyes of the ostrich are large and very keen, enabling them to discern objects at a great distance. Their hearing also is remarkably acute. I have been told that the sight of a horse inspires them with great terror, and that a gentleman recently rode one of these animals within view from their inclosure at Anaheim, when the birds, catching sight of him, were thrown into such fright that the rider was forced to remove him. Their cry is loud and piercing, and may be heard at a great distance. "When contending with a foe they hiss vigorously, thus publishing their relationship to the goose."

The feathers of the ostrich are taken chiefly from the tail and wings. Those of the males are either white or brown, tipped with black, and are remarkable for their length. It is for these long plumes mainly that the ostrich is farmed. The feathers of the female are dark brown, mingled with white. For centuries past the handsome plumes of the African ostrich have been worn by men as insignia of their rank. The badge of the present Prince of Wales is three white ostrich feathers. When John, of Luxembourg, was defeated at Crecy, by Edward the Black Prince, he wore in his casque one of their long, white plumes. And, even prior to that date, they distinguished the house of Plantaganet. The wearing of three feathers, grouped, in the coronet of an English prince is said to have been introduced by Henry, eldest son of James the First. Certain young women of America must have adopted the fashion, for, seated in front of me at church last Sunday morning, was a young lady with three white plumes set against the front of her hat, its only trimming.

Anaheim is one of the oldest of recent settlements in Southern California, having been established nearly twenty-five years ago. It was settled by a colony of Germans, who planted extensively the "wine grape," introduced by the Spanish missionaries. In a few years they were freely engaged in the manufacture of wine. They made money at the baleful business, and laid it up, as is so natural for the frugal Teuton to do, instead of expending it in making their surroundings beautiful. And, now, in their plain and exteriorly comfortable homes, they appear to be taking their ease. A few of the residences are very pretty. The place has a drowsy, Autumnish look. No new buildings are going up. There is no activity in the streets. The spirit of enterprise seems to have taken its flight, if it were ever here. Anaheim is at the midnight of a long sleep. When it wakens it will find that the enterprising villages of Orange, Tustin, and Santa Ana have far outstripped it in the race for business and improvement.

Leaving here we pass on to the last-named town, one of five charming villages occupying the valley of the Santa Ana River, seven miles south-east of Anaheim, two-and-a-half miles south of Orange, with Tustin on the east, and Westminster, a neat, thriving town, founded by a colony of enterprising temperance people, who at the beginning forever barred out the saloon by proviso in their act of incorporation, lying due south of it.

Tustin and Orange are little more than collections of beautiful homes, with a post-office, grocery, hotel, store, church, and school-house located at the center, while the country adjacent presents a net-work of vineyards and orchards of all sorts. Access to these places is by carriage.

## SANTA ANA.

Every rod of the ride is delightful. Long lines of eucalypti, pepper, and cypress trees grace the road on either side. The gates of the pretty yards stand invitingly open. The hedges are trim and green. Flowers brighten the closely cut lawns. The cottages, of a dozen chaste styles, look cool and inviting on this warm afternoon. Every thing betokens prosperity. Still, so recently were none of these things here, that their existence seems like the work of magic.

Santa Ana, the largest of the group, contains about two thousand five hundred people. Eleven years ago its now vine-clad site was a treeless waste, a mere pasture for flocks. Its inhabitants were principally Mexicans, and widely scattered. But its climate had become known as one in which consumptives were almost sure to recover. Word to that effect reached Minnesota and other Northwestern States. Hither from them came numbers of that class of invalids. Few of them could come alone. So with them came the strong and well, bringing some money, indomitable energy, and power to scheme and drive. Mr. J. W. Layman, of Minneapolis, one of the first on the ground, built a hotel. Then followed church and school-house. Soon up sprang lodges of Masons, Odd Fellows

Good Templars, a Band of Hope, and a Post of the Grand Army of the Republic. All wide-awake in their legitimate fields of activity, and now possessing their own inviting halls for meetings. Transplanting their love of refinement into the new soil, the citizens foster art in several of its departments, and pay liberal stipends to teachers.

From the Santa Ana River and the two strata, sheets, or lakes of water which underlie the entire plain, one at a depth of sixty, the other at a distance of three hundred feet, is derived the water supply for this coterie of settlements. For domestic purposes the fluid is obtained through artesian wells, sunk to the second stratum. To sum up, the three strong points of the region are: An almost faultless climate, a wonderfully fertile soil, an inexhaustible supply of pure, cold water.

Eight miles south of Santa Ana lies Newport Bay, the most accessible sea-side resort. In full view from it, and near enough for an enjoyable sail, are the islands of San Clemente and Santa Catalina, notable for their scenic charms and historical associations.

Something like a mile below Santa Ana, on property belonging to one Captain West, are to be seen the ruins of an old adobe house, which, you will be told, was the birthplace of the famous Mexican General and President, Santa Anna. But history robs the place of this honor. A friend, familiar with every page of the man's career, informs me that the Mexican President never saw California. Antonio Lopez was a native of the State of Jalapa, Mexico. At one time in his life he was the proprietor of a handsome estate in that republic, which, out of gratitude for the services of Sant Anne, he named Santa Anna. There being other men in Mexico of the name of Lopez, he in time came to be designated as Lopez de Santa Anna; and, later, by the American newspapers, and also by the American army during the war with Mexico, as General, then President Santa Anna. To this river and valley the name Santa Ana was given by the "Missionary Fathers" during their first journey from San Diego to Monterey, and long before the day of Lopez, of Jalapa.

## XVII.

## A Singular Character.

LAST Tuesday afternoon it was arranged by the lovely woman to whom belongs this hill-top home, that I should next day accompany her on a visit to a floral garden lying just within the western limits of the city, and of which one Peter Ramau, a native of Hungary, and a singular specimen of the *genus homo*, is the proprietor. The day proved a delightful one. Overhead nothing but blue; in the sunlight an indescribable charm; an attraction which fairly drew people out of doors, and when out, produced in them a feeling of happiness and exultation. In no other spot on this continent have I experienced this exhilarating effect of the sunlight. But here ordinarily are to be enjoyed months of such days every year—days when you are very pleased, and hardly know why.

Taking a main street car to the Washington Gardens, two miles from the center of town, we were within twenty minutes walk of the premises. Both florists and their grounds are plentiful in this part of the country, and I write of this man only because

## A SINGULAR CHARACTER. 123

he is an odd pattern of humanity, after which few mortals are fashioned in any land. These persons seem to be freaks of nature; made up of mismatched material; an assorted lot; deviations from the normal plan; people remarkable only for their eccentricities. Occasionally I pass such persons on the street here. In the veins of most of them flows the blood of two races, and sometimes of more. Usually their appearance is so striking that one is eager to see them again. Not a few of them are women. I call to mind one who is of immediate French, English, and Hawaiian descent. The characteristics of the three races are very marked in her. Strange vicissitudes have crowded themselves into her life. Born on the Atlantic; reared and educated in England; connected with well-known families, both in that country and France; a resident of this coast for forty years; several times the possessor of great wealth, and as many times the subject of absolute want, she has yet, under all circumstances, been a woman of influence, and of great charity, bestowed often upon the most lowly. She speaks Spanish, Hawaiian, English, and some French. There are enough interesting facts connected with her history to fill volumes.

Peter Ramau met us at the rude gate in front

of his home, opened it politely, and inquired: "Are you tired, ladies?"

Mrs. H—, who had made several visits to the place, and knew the man quite well, replied: "It costs your friends something to visit yourself and your flowers, Mr. Ramau."

"Yes; and I 'm so much obliged to them for coming. Rest a little on the porch, and then I 'll show you what Madame Nature can do at flower making."

The man has a large round head, is broad-chested, and of medium height. His eyes sparkle with pleasure when he smiles, but flash like flames when he is angry, or some unwelcome thought of the past flits through his mind. His brain seems to be crowded with strange conceits and fancies. A reference to the beauty of his flowers is sure to cause these odd notions to spring into the queerest unions, like the bits of glass in a kaleidoscope. His manner is kindly and his disposition humane. Religiously he is a ship with anchor gone. He loves birds, dogs, and flowers passionately. His wife is dead. Two grown sons constitute the human part of his family.

In front and to the right of his rambling and desolate adobe house lies his flower garden, a parallelogram containing two acres or less. No other florist on earth ever arranged a garden spot like that. It is disarranged like the owner's brain, and strange to say, the disorder in both is one of their chief attractions. Will the reader try to imagine a small patch of anemones, beautiful beyond the power of pen to describe, springing out of a larger plat of verbenas, dense, gay with bloom? Then think of more anemones waving on the top of their long, slender stems, among thorny rose bushes and woody heliotrope; and of more still, crowded by azure forget-me-nots and French pinks of every hue. See tulips as large as tea-cups, single, double, mottled, striped, ringed, and bordered, with a dozen glorious colors, trying to get the upper hand of fragrant thyme and rank geraniums. Here, they are reaching out for sunlight from under small orange trees; there, from amid bushy fuchsias.

Bending over a cluster of anemones, simply matchless for the delicacy, variety, and brilliancy of their colors, Mr. Ramau clasped a dozen of the perfect cups with both hands, and looking up in my face, said, solemnly:

"Do you know, madam, I see God in these. I can't see him in the Bible. If God were to tell me, this day, that in a year I must die, do you know what I would do?"—tears glistened in the man's eyes—"I would go to work and collect every variety of anemone under heaven, and get them to blooming in my ground. Then I'd watch them and admire them down to the last hour. Ah! madam, the anemone is God's flower. Only look! Where can you find such a sight?"

I did look, and could myself have cried over the flowers. They seemed almost human, almost able to think and love. There swayed to-and-fro splendid cups of scarlet, crimson, maroon, deep red, rich orange, soft pink, and delicate straw-color; cups of blue, cups of purple and yellow, in shades magnificent. Some were single, others were double. As in the case of the tulips, the man had taxed his skill to the uttermost to produce these marvelous tints.

"Are you aware, madam," he continued, "that it is the multitude and variety of anemones in the gardens of Francis Joseph, of Austria, that make them so famous? My! madam, it is heaven to walk there. There you can see beds four hundred feet long, containing ever variety of wind-flower in the world, and all collected for the enjoyment of the people."

We remarked: "It is a pity you can not see

God in the Bible, since he there speaks more to the purpose on some points than in flowers."

"Never mind; I see him in these gems of his. But now mark what man can do. Of anemones and tulips God made just one variety. Man, taking that beginning, has, by his skill, multiplied the varieties until now they are endless, and so beautiful! Madam, that's man. And God does n't even make them grow. Man does that. I tell you, there's a deal of God in man."

"Man is evidently your God," we replied. "Can you make a plant drink, draw sustenance from the soil, extract oxygen from the air, or appropriate sunlight?" Just then two ladies entered the grounds, and he turned to meet them.

During our stay we had observed numerous dogs lying under the trees, and playing about the house, and on his return we inquired if he owned them.

"Yes; they are my family. Let me call them together, that you may see them. I have seventeen in all."

He was then patting the heads of two that were impatiently pulling at his garments, just as I have seen peevish children tug at a mother's clothing. Now he began calling, whistling, shouting for his family. "Lucy! Lucy! Here, Hongkong! here, brave fellow! Hongkong, madam, is a Chinese dog. Pat! here Pat! Pat is from green Erin, ladies, and does n't like the English."

Thus the man invited and coaxed until six or eight remarkable specimens of the canine race were wildly racing around him, leaping upon his person, or licking his hands, and all apparently anxious to know why they had been called together.

"Now, would you like to hear them sing? Shall I show you that some dogs know more than some men?"

"If dogs can do any thing more human than to bark and bite, we should be interested in seeing them do it," we answered.

Thereupon, his eyes lighting up, he began to hum a lively tune. Instantly the animals broke into canine bass, tenor, alto, soprano, and all kept time with their leader. When the time quickened, they leaped upon him, sprang into the air, whined, barked, howled. Every dog was in a perfect frenzy, and we were in bedlam. Hongkong, a splendid greyhound, turned his back toward his master, stretched his long nose out toward the sky, and struck into a woeful, piercing cry, followed by a low, melancholy wail. The creature's heart seemed broken. He was telling his grief to the invisible stars. His whole aspect betokened the deepest sorrow. The scene and the noise beggared description. I doubt if any thing like it could be witnessed outside of Southern California, where scenes and objects unequaled are the rule rather than the exception.

We endured the horrible din five minutes, perhaps ten, and then entreated the strange man to bring that most unique of all vocal concerts to a close. But the dogs were proud of their accomplishments, and were far less ready to end the performance than to begin it. By degrees, however, quiet was restored.

Then said the Hungarian: "Ladies, until recently I have kept two hundred mocking-birds. The food of the happy songsters cost me ten dollars every week. At last I concluded that was an expensive amusement for a poor man. So one day I opened the cages and gave the sweet singers their freedom. You see a few cages still, with here and there a captive, but the family numbers only fifteen now. I love nature, and could n't live a day without these dogs, and birds, and anemones. Like that lovely woman "—meaning Mrs. H—, whose snowy hair, pleasant eyes, and fair complexion attract notice wherever she goes—" they show me how God loves beautiful things.

"Madame, I never go to bed at night without taking a long, loving look at the stars; nor rise in the morning without indulging in a tender chat with the beauties in my garden. I tell you, if I but had money to buy a telescope, I'd spend the nights in taking flights among the stars, and during the day I'd grow toward heaven among my flowers.

"Where was I born? In Vodena, Hungary, a land which General Fremont declares is the 'most beautiful under the sun,' and he has seen it. For several years I was an officer in the Austrian army. In 1850 I fled to this country. I married in Iowa. My wife died in 1869, leaving me two good sons. Louie lives here with me. My real name you must not know. The Austrian Government has searched for me all over these United States."

It was drawing towards sunset, and other parties arriving, Mrs. H— and myself strolled for a moment through the trim orange orchard in the rear of the house. The handsome trees were laden with fragrant blossoms and ripe fruit. Beyond this stretched a vineyard of considerable size and in fine condition. The dresser of these grounds is Louie Ramau, one of the sons. Returning, we bade the father good-bye and walked away, wondering if there were on the earth another mortal like him.

## XVIII.

## "THE NATIVE CALIFORNIANS."

IN his book entitled "Three Years in California," the Rev. Walter Colton talks much about the "native Californians," and in terms which leave most readers in doubt whether he means the Spaniards who centuries ago invaded California, or the Indian races whom the Spaniards found here. The latter are grouped by Mr. Hubert H. Bancroft under three divisions, called, "The Northern, Central, and Southern Californians." These, then, were the native Californians at the time of the Spanish invasion, but not the native Californians of Mr. Colton's book. Fully two centuries before the acquirement of California by the United States, the Spaniards had spread over Central America, Mexico, and California—then a part of Mexico. They not only subdued the Indian tribes or nations inhabiting these countries, but married, traded, and lived among them, and had possession of their soil. Thus, as the years passed on and on, there sprang up a nation in whose veins flowed a mixture of

Spanish and Indian blood, and which spoke the Spanish language, corrupted, in many instances, by words and phrases from the vocabularies of the vanquished peoples.

Also, after Mexico threw off the Spanish yoke—some years prior to the obtaining of California by our government—considerable colonies from that country settled on this part of the coast. They, likewise, were of Spanish and native origin, and spoke the Spanish tongue. From these two sources, then, come the "native Californians" with whom we mingle to-day, and of Mr. Colton's acquaintance from 1846 to 1849. In other words: Before they became Americans, by our acquiring their territory, they were Mexicans, and by that term are they very generally designated here to-day. Tourists and others often refer to them as Castilians, using the "pure Castilian tongue." But the fact is, few, if any of them, ever saw Spain. Much less were they born in Castile. However, some of them are of full Spanish blood, and are intelligent and meritorious citizens. Proverbial for politeness and generosity, often too confiding for their own interests, and always ready to serve a friend to the uttermost, they of course soon win the high esteem of the English-speaking Americans. Almost without exception they are members of the Catholic Church.

On the contrary, the lower orders of Mexicans are exceedingly illiterate, but their condition in this respect is said to be due not so much to incapacity as to neglect. "It must be remembered," says an educated missionary who has for years labored among them, "that their religion is the Roman Catholic, mingled still, in too many cases, with traces of the ancient worship of the original tribes. Owing to the disposition of the Catholic Church to temporize with its Indian converts, as it did with the heathen nations brought into its fold in Constantine's day, they were allowed to retain certain of their old observances. From that day to this the Catholic Church has been their teacher, and, as might be expected, the lower Mexican element of our population to-day, is, in a religious sense, elevated not far above its Indian ancestors prior to the Spanish conquest."

It should be remembered that those who do break away from the Catholic Church, among this class of Californians, seem to take most cordially to the denominations whose forms of worship differ most from the showy services of the system under which they have grown up. Many of them enter the Presbyterian fold, where they find neither images, crucifixes, lighted candles, holy fire, holy water, the confessional, nor vestments for the ministry.

"I can not express to you," said an intelligent Mexican, who had been reared in the Romish Church, but who is now a Protestant, "how distasteful to me, for years, was the sight of a clergyman in robes. And usually, according to my observation, when a Catholic becomes dissatisfied with that system, he flees to the one farthest removed from it, or to none at all."

At three points in Los Angeles County Mexican Presbyterian churches have been established, the stronger organization being in this city. No Sunday-schools are conducted as yet, but a day school is in progress at Anaheim and in Los Angeles.

There are now few Mexican families living in affluence in Southern California. Formerly many were rich in lands and herds, but upon the accession of the territory, understanding neither our language nor our laws, they were soon involved in endless litigations with rapacious fortune-hunters from "the States," who had managed, by one means or another, to secure claims upon their property. Often in these cases the decisions of the Federal courts were adverse to the Mexicans, how, or why, the latter could not tell, and in an incredibly short time numbers found themselves face to face with poverty. Unaccustomed to work, few were able to retrieve their condition, and in their straits actually borrowed money of the robbers at a ruinous interest, and mortgaging, to secure its payment, whatever property they had left. Of course this step hastened the end. Finally, realizing that they were no match for the new proprietors of the soil, many became disheartened, "gave themselves up to melancholy," and erelong moved into narrow homes on which there were no mortgages.

"When I first came here, eleven years ago," said a lady this morning, "there were Mexicans everywhere. They lounged on door-steps, within the presidios of their homes, in front of the shops and stores, and along the country roads. Apparently without a care, they laughed, chatted, and danced. Now, I meet a few on the streets as I go about the city, but their number seems greatly diminished. Doubtless some of them have caught the spirit of thrift and enterprise possessed by our people, and have adopted habits of industry; but my opinion is that the race is giving way before the Americans, whose force and tenacity of life are so much greater."

The Mexican women are objects of great interest to me. On the street the middle-aged woman appears almost invariably in a dress of black, destitute of trimmings. The skirt is made of straight breadths, minus any thing like drapery. Upon her head, framing in her swarthy face, she wears, usually, a plain black shawl folded cornerwise, and held together under her chin by her ungloved hand. She never carries parasol or umbrella, even though the Summer sun, holding the mercury up to 100° in the shade, beats down upon her head, cooking her ideas and wrinkling her skin. There she goes! hair, eyes, shawl, dress, the color of night; in her face no brightness; a silent figure, destined to be left behind by a people whose skill, and power, and range of knowledge simply bewilder her.

Many of the younger women strongly resemble each other, with their black hair, dark eyes, southern complexion, medium height, slender figure, and cheerful, animated countenance. They dress in colors and with taste, and walk with an elastic step. But, a few years hence, should they follow in the course of their mothers, their forms will lose their compactness and shapeliness. Their carriage will become slow and heavy. American gentlemen frequently marry daughters of the better families, and our young women occasionally take husbands from among the educated Mexicans. So far as I have been able to learn, these unions prove quite as happy as if formed with persons of the same race. Having occasion the other day to call at the city home of Don Pio Pico, the last Mexican governor of California, I found there a niece of that courtly gentleman, from Santa Barbara. She was a ladylike, beautiful-looking little woman, who spoke English nicely, having enjoyed the benefit of the American schools in that city. Some time before she had married a young Mr. Perkins, from the East, with whom she seemed to be much pleased, and I could see no reason why he should not be pleased with her.

On another occasion, when taking a walk in the outskirts of the city, after a hard day's work, I came upon one of the early rural homes of Los Angeles. The house stood far back from the street, in the midst of an orange-grove, and was a many-roomed adobe, built out this way and that, with a wide veranda running around most of it, and all the apartments opening upon that. It was the famous Wolfskill residence. William Wolfskill was a Kentuckian, I believe, who wandered off to this coast and "built this house over fifty years ago." He has gone to his rest, but the place is occupied by a son, whose wife is a beautiful Spanish woman. Entering the open gateway, and following the drive to the house, I found Mrs. Wolfskill seated on the veranda, surrounded by a half-dozen children, all evidently of Spanish descent, all busy doing something, and apparently having a good time. Rising as I drew near, she greeted me kindly, using excellent English. I have seldom seen a more attractive woman. A wealth of dark hair was coiled loosely upon the top of her head. Her manners were charming, and I noticed that her toilet had been made without the use of cosmetics, a feature of dress which seems to be very popular among the young women of the Spanish tongue.

Upon my inquiring if the whole group of little ones were hers, she replied: "Ah, no! I wish they were. It is the sorrow of my life that I have not such a family of children. I love them, and find great pleasure in caring for them. The babe only is mine." After chatting a little time, and the evening shadows beginning to fall, I bade her good-night, having enjoyed the call. Afterward I learned that the lady represents the best class of Spanish-speaking people on the coast. For that reason I mention the trifling incident of my call.

## XIX.

## SCHOOLS OF LOS ANGELES.

NORMAL SCHOOL—LADIES' COLLEGE—STATE UNIVERSITY, AND MAGNETIC OBSERVATORY.

FOR twelve years Los Angeles has supported an excellent system of public schools. Although the city covers a large area, school-houses are conveniently located in every part. Many of the buildings are new, thoroughly equipped for their purpose, and are attractive externally. And it is doubtful if in any city of its size there can be found a body of teachers better qualified. Indeed the city is reputed for the high scholarship of the teachers in the graded schools. Moreover, the State itself demands unusual accomplishments in the candidates for certificates. It has been said that eastern teachers of experience have sometimes failed to pass the examinations it requires. A principal in one of the schools has just stated that applicants for certificates must pass an examination in a number of branches not demanded in other States. He must be familiar with the school laws of California, and have an intelligent acquaintance with the State Constitution.

A branch of the State Normal School is making fine headway here under Professor Ira More as principal. Accompanied by this gentleman and Mrs. More, on a recent Wednesday, the writer took a look through the great Normal School building, and paid some attention to the methods of instruction. It may truthfully be said that, from basement to roof, the structure is one of the best lighted, best ventilated, and most economically arranged, I have ever seen for the purpose. It is a handsome edifice, built of brick, is three stories in height, has spacious halls, ample class-rooms, and enough of them, a sunny office for the principal, a bright parlor for the preceptress, an inviting library on the first floor, partially filled with helpful books, and a well-equipped laboratory in the basement. In this latter room the professor of chemistry, Miss Sarah P. Monks, an alumnus of Vassar College, becomes a Michael Faraday every afternoon to a class of shrewd, inquiring young men and women. In the cheerful chapel, commanding a broad outlook westward, down the rich Cahuenga Valley, I found assembled for the simple religious exercises of the morning, nearly two hundred pupils in training for the teacher's profession. They were an earnest, sensible-looking company of students, evidently not at school for play, and represented a half-dozen nationalities, I should judge. Their free and frequent questions upon the subjects under study in the class-rooms, afterward, showed they were working for a purpose.

The Normal-school building crowns a commanding eminence between Bunker Hill Avenue and Charity Street, and has the distinction of being the only school of its class in the United States, which is located in the midst of an orange grove. The art of the landscape gardener is now converting the formerly rough hill-side in front of it, into a picture wherein mingle flowers, trees, terraces, a fountain, and graveled drives. Glancing in any direction from the windows of the building, or from its high tower, the views of the country are inspiring. In the east loom up the stately Sierra Madre Mountains. On the west and north-west rise the Santa Monica and San Fernando chains, their sides chiseled with the storms of centuries, while towards the south stretches the verdant Los Angeles valley, bordered, twenty miles away, by a strip of the sea. All around lives the city, busy, taking on greater vigor every day. How could intelligent young men and women be otherwise than in earnest, while fitting themselves for life's work, amid such scenes?

Westward, a distance of three miles, or less, stands the "University of Southern California," founded by the Methodists in 1878. Its curriculum is open to both sexes. The institution is a thriving one, occupies a fine building, and holds the title to considerable real estate. It has the confidence of the community, and looks forward to success. An important department of this University, is the Chaffey College of Horticulture, located at Ontario, the model colony of Southern California.

Now turn your eye toward that lovely elevation lying to the north-west of the Normal School, and possibly a mile distant. The handsome structure you see, built in the composite style, so much in favor just now, is Ellis Villa College, a school for young ladies, built and opened in 1884 by Rev. John Ellis, then pastor of the First Presbyterian Church of Los Angeles, but now the president of the college. The building overlooks scenery as varied as that seen from the Normal School. The grounds are charmingly improved. Every young woman privileged to pursue her course of study in the presence of so much that is noble and beautiful in nature, ought to form a character as attractive as the scenes she looks upon.

About the time the Ellis Villa School opened its doors, there was established at Hermosa Vista Hill, a delightful eminence lying between the city of Los Angeles and the village of Pasadena, the "Eden of Southern California," a college for young men, also under the auspices of the Presbyterian Church, but not intended to be sectarian. Dr. Ellis was one of the prime movers in the enterprise. When projected, both these schools were by many thought to be far in advance of the necessities in the line of education, because in advance of the population necessary to sustain them. But the cautious ones could not foresee, that in the short space of three years the metropolis of Southern California would double the number of its inhabitants, and that the increase of population in the county would preserve a fair proportion to that of the city, thus creating a demand for institutions of this class. On their arrival here, now, settlers find well planted and at work, every grade of school, from the kindergarten to the university.

The College of Hermosa Vista Hill is as favored as those I have described for scenic surroundings, being seated almost under the shadows of the Sierra

Madre, with the fair San Gabriel valley spread out on one side. Here, surely, young men may prepare to live for their country, if not to die for it.

I learn this morning that the Baptists and Episcopalians are soon to appear on the field, bidding for their share of patronage for schools of a high order. Thus about all the ground will be occupied, and the children of all denominations may hurry forward. Teachers, books, and desks will be ready for them.

Now if the reader is not weary, we will retrace our steps to the fine, sloping ground in the rear of the Normal School. Here, built into the hill-side, and half hidden by the orange trees, we shall find an institution of an entirely different, but most interesting character. This is an "observatory for determining the direction, variation, and force of the magnetic current." It is the only observatory of the kind in the United States, and the best one in the world. There are in this country several other stations where partial or occasional observations of the magnetic current are made. But here the record is ceaseless. The work of the needles stops night nor day, for holy day nor holiday. Here is one kind of perpetual motion. The officer whom the government appoints to duty in this dark, double-walled mite of a structure, is little better than buried. Unless he has an assistant, competent and faithful, he has no hours off. The magnetic current knows no Sunday. It furnishes a man no tent on the sea-shore for a three weeks' vacation in Summer.

The officer now in charge of this observatory is Charles C. Terry, Jr., of Columbus, Georgia, and is a relative—cousin, if I am correct—of General Terry, of Fort Fisher fame. The reader remembers that General Terry distinguished himself by carrying that stronghold by assault, after General B. F. Butler, co-operating with Admiral Porter, in an unsuccessful attempt to capture the fort, declared it could not be taken. Charles Terry is a young man, thirty years of age, perhaps, and though very courteous and obliging, seldom admits a visitor inside his castle, especially if he lacks the intelligence to comprehend its purpose and machinery. The writer was fortunate in having a "friend at court," and got in.

After our glance at the teaching of all sorts of sciences at the Normal School, Mrs. More and myself concluded we should like to see the inside of a building so rare as is this observatory, and to learn how the changes made by that mysterious force, magnetism, are recorded. Professor More, therefore, accompanied us down the narrow board walk leading to the little hut in the ground, and as we approached the door, said:

"Ladies, you'd better wait outside until I see if you can be admitted." Then, with a firm, steady push, he turned the solid outer door on its hinges, and with a slow and cautious step, lest he should jar the magnetic needles, so faithfully at work in their dark dungeon, entered the narrow passage separating the inner from the outer wall, and disappeared. Meanwhile, we who were in waiting, speculated as to the things within, and questioned if it were possible to tread lightly enough not to cause the delicate instruments to break the ninth commandment. In a short time our friend emerged, saying:

"Mr. Terry is busy performing a difficult piece of work, which must not be laid aside. But he says that if you will call again in a half-hour you will be welcome, and he will take pleasure in explaining to you how man, by his wonderful inventions, has compelled the magnetic current to disclose some of the laws by which it is governed."

We all returned to the school building, where Mrs. More and myself passed the half-hour list-

## THE MAGNETIC OBSERVATORY. 147

ening to a specimen of able teaching of grammar. Then returning to the observatory, we pushed open the massive door, closed it softly behind us, groped our way along the dark hall until we came to a door made partly of glass, and through which fell a faint light. Upon our rapping gently, it was instantly opened by Mr. Terry, in shirt-sleeves and long apron, the latter made of striped ticking, and covering him from the neck down.

Greeting us kindly, he immediately defined the work of the observatory to be: "The photographing on paper, and afterwards making them permanent by chemical processes, the direction, changes, dip, and inclination of the magnetic current."

He then spent some moments explaining the use of certain appliances of his work-room, as a sort of introduction to our next lesson. Then asking us to resign our steel-ribbed umbrellas to the care of his chemicals, and charging us to step lightly, he led the way to a small, double-walled, windowless inner room, the walls of which were black with smoke from burning lamps. Admitting us first, he followed and carefully closed the door. Here, each under a small glass dome covered with black cloth, were three magnetic needles, suspended by delicate cords. One of them indicating the vertical force, another the horizontal force, and the third the dip and inclination of the current of terrestrial magnetism. These needles are seldom, if ever, absolutely at rest. Their *movements* are photographed by light obtained from three coal-oil lamps, kept always burning. The light is focalized by small mirrors, upon strips of white paper, placed in an upright cylinder, itself incased in dark cloth. Mr. Terry explained, in a clear and interesting way, the manner in which all this work is done. But I forbear attempting the task here, lest the words I should use might shock those nicely hung needles into recording a great deviation of the magnetic current. Should the reader ever visit Los Angeles let him pay a visit to the Normal School, where Professor More will make him welcome, and then walk down to the observatory and take a look at it. There is little hope of his getting inside, but it is a satisfaction to say one has seen the place.

However, should you gain admission into that strange inner room, you will probably be required to leave behind you, not your umbrellas only, but your gold rings, watches, the metallic buttons on your clothing, and, if you are a woman, your hoop-skirts and corsets, if they have steels in them. All these things will so attract the magnets towards you as to make them fail in their duty to the government. To some extent Mrs. More and myself were so appareled, but Mr. Terry politely said that, instead of asking us to lay the articles aside, he would, in his report for that day, state the cause of the aberration of the magnets, that the blame might not be charged to the magnetic current.

Upon my return to Los Angeles last October, after an absence of two years on the northern part of the coast, I learned that Mr. Terry, failing in health, contemplated resigning his position. His misfortune was thought by his friends to be due to two causes—close confinement in the observatory, and excessive smoking. To smoke, therefore, is one thing which the magnetic force allows a man to do. None the less, he makes a mistake who does it. They said Mr. Terry "smoked for company." If there is a place in the world where the practice would be justified on that ground, that little hut in the ground is the one.

## XX.

## A NOBLE PIONEER.

FOR some years preceding, as well as subsequent to, the accession of California, there figured on the Pacific Coast many remarkable characters. Among them, besides native Californians, were Americans from every quarter of the Union, and also representatives of every nation on the globe. Some of them were brave, upright men, loyal as friends, generous to a fault, incapable of an unmanly deed. Others were unprincipled, mercenary, and placed a low value upon human life. To commit crime seemed as natural to them as to breathe. Of these some sprang from an ignoble ancestry. In others the bad blood seemed to start with themselves; but ill-doing distinguished them all. Society lived in terror of them, and slept peacefully only when the earth was rounded above their graves. But one by one both classes have left the stage, until to-day a survivor is met only here and there. Of one of these survivors, ranking in the first category, I have occasion to speak in this chapter.

Colonel J. J. Warner, now an active octogenarian, has resided in this part of the Golden State for fifty-six years. These years embrace the most interesting and most exciting period in the modern history of California. In the stirring scenes attending the transfer of the Territory to the United States, as in the more turbulent and rancorous ones of the late Civil War, when wide difference of opinion as to the right of the government to coerce the slaveholding States divided the citizens of the coast, Colonel Warner was no inconsiderable figure. Fearless, resolute, absolutely loyal to the government, he stood a steadfast advocate of the Union, when the fiery adherents of secession, by whom the State was thronged, were determined to carry California for the Confederacy. Colonel Warner lived long also in the midst of treacherous Indian tribes, where a moment's hesitation, in exigent cases, would have proved fatal to his own and others' priceless interests. More than once his prompt action in great danger saved human lives and property.

Thus for many years following his settlement in Los Angeles were the circumstances of his life such as to bring out the strong traits in his character.

Such men, living in such times, usually make

bitter enemies; but of this venerable pioneer, not one of the surviving zealous partisans of to-day speaks in other than terms of friendship and respect. Not a tongue is barbed with enmity. And if general testimony be accepted, none have won greater respect for their opinions, or higher appreciation of their worth, than has the subject of this sketch, the first president of the California Historical Society.

Colonel Warner is a native of Lyme, Connecticut, in which place he was born in the year 1807. His ancestors were early settlers in that part of the State, and were persons of influence. His maternal grandfather, Samuel Selden, was a colonel in Washington's army when the colonial force evacuated New York. Colonel Warner is himself a favorite uncle of the wife of Chief-Justice Waite. He is a cousin of the wife of the eminent Judge Ranney, of Cleveland, Ohio. Other of his relatives scattered over the Buckeye State are quite numerous. Among them is President C. C. Waite, of the Cincinnati, Hamilton and Dayton Railway. Probably a half-century has passed since one of these friends has grasped the hand of the esteemed pioneer.

In October, 1830, Mr. Warner, being then twenty-three years of age, and of frail constitution, left Connecticut to seek health and fortune in the "far

West." Arriving in St. Louis early in December, he there made the acquaintance of Jedediah S. Smith, a famous member of the Rocky Mountain Fur Company. The noted trapper had just come into the bustling village from the North-west, with an invoice of furs. He was accompanied by his partners, Jackson and the Soublette brothers. Young Warner's imagination was excited by their stirring accounts of trapper life, and he concluded that rough fare and mountain air were just the things required to render him strong and vigorous. So, seeking an interview with the intrepid Smith, he conferred with him in reference to spending a limited time at his camps in the distant mountains. The hardy trapper discouraged the step, and the tall New England youth had to content himself with spending the Winter in the "metropolis of Missouri." However, when the Spring opened, Mr. Smith, who also had remained in St. Louis, offered him a position in an expedition he was organizing to convey a quantity of merchandise to Santa Fe, and once there, Mr. Warner might choose between remaining in the capital of New Mexico and returning East for a fresh stock of goods. Smith himself headed the enterprise, but not long after reaching Santa Fe he met his death at the hands of Indians on the Semeron River. This blow broke up the operations of his firm in New Mexico. Mr. Jackson wound up their affairs, and in company with his young friend Warner started on the perilous overland journey to Southern California, crossing the great desert of which considerable has already been said in this volume, and arrived in Los Angeles in November, 1831.

A few months subsequently Mr. Warner, desirous of seeing something of the vast North-west, joined a hunting party bound to the San Joaquin River and its tributaries, to the Sacramento and its branches, and thence northward to the mouth of the Umpqua River in Oregon, and from that point eastward to the Klamath Lake region. In this then long and perilous trip, the young man accomplished his earnest desire to take life roughly for awhile. The adventures of the party were numerous, and some of them trying, if not exciting. For the fatigue and hardship he cared little, if he might but take his share in the risks and perils, and in the end turn out a Hercules in strength. And this he did, if the stories now told of his subsequent almost incredible feats of horsemanship, and of his ability to cope with a score of armed assailants, be true.

In those early days, trapping beaver in the great

mountain ranges of the West was an exciting pursuit. Young men eager to engage in it were never lacking. All California was traversed by parties of bold hunters, who, upon carrying their furs to market in the East, set afloat marvelous accounts of the fair land. Twenty years later there were residing in Oregon, Washington, and California, numbers of men, of distinguished endowments, who had served an apprenticeship in trapping; men who had been attached to the hazardous business, fascinated by the wild, independent life they led. But the country settling up, one after another, for various reasons, abandoned the mountains and took up his residence on the coast. Some turned their attention to civil affairs, and have rendered excellent service to the Pacific States.

Returning to Los Angeles after an absence of fourteen months, Mr. Warner settled permanently in Southern California. He was now twenty-seven years of age. Three years later, 1837, he was united in marriage to a young lady who was the ward of Don Pio Pico, then administrator of the Mission of San Luis Rey, and afterward Mexican governor of California. The mother of the young woman being dead, her father had placed her at school in this mission. When the marriage took place, Mr. Pico acted as godfather of the groom, in obedience to a requirement of the Catholic Church, I believe. Out of this relation sprang an attachment between the two young men, which has known no change through fifty eventful years. Mr. Pico, of whom something is said further on in this volume, is now a resident of this city. He has seen upwards of eighty years, and is a person of striking appearance.

Mr. and Mrs. Warner established their home in Los Angeles, where they resided for a considerable period, and here occurred one of the incidents which attest the man's courage, and exemplify his fidelity to his friends.

During the Mexican *régime* in California, local rebellions were frequent on the coast. Factions out of power were ever plotting to unseat those in authority. The city of Los Angeles was sometimes the theater for this sort of pastime, and one morning Mr. Warner found himself suddenly and innocently taking part in one of these *émeutes*. The conflict began and ended so quickly, however, that it seemed more like a whiff of air off a battle-field than like a genuine struggle. When it was passed the hero found himself the possessor of a broken arm and needing the help of a surgeon.

Upon throwing open their dwellings early one sunny morning in April, I forget what year, the citizens of Los Angeles were surprised to see a company of armed soldiers encamped on their plaza, as a convenient point for operations in any direction. The commander of the body was one Espinosa, an adherent of the then reigning governor, Alvarado. The purpose of his silent and secret entrance into the city was the arrest of certain prominent men suspected of disaffection toward Alvarado, and of conspiring to reinstate in the gubernatorial chair one Corrillio, previously deposed from that office. Among the suspected persons were Don Pio Pico and his brother, Andrez Pico, subsequently quite a notable character in the history of Southern California, and a search for these parties had already begun.

Colonel and Mrs. Warner were seated at the breakfast table, in a cozy room at the rear of his store, when an authoritative knock upon the front door caused the husband to spring to his feet. Upon opening the door there confronted him a number of Espinosa's men, who inquired if Don Pio Pico were there. They were courteously informed that he was not. Not satisfied, they proposed to search the premises, a privilege which was at once refused.

This provoked an attempt to arrest the proprietor, who stoutly resisted. A hand-to-hand struggle ensued, and the parties were soon struggling in the street, immediately below where the St. Charles and St. Elmo hotels now stand. At this juncture Espinosa himself appeared, coming out of Commercial Street, with his revolver drawn. Perceiving him, Colonel Warner realized his danger, and with great force breaking away from his assailants, he made a dash upon that officer, and wrested the weapon from his hand. Soon after, having occasion to use his left arm, he found it would not obey his will. In the struggle to quickly free himself from his captors, one of them, intending to disable him, had by an instantaneous blow broken the arm between the shoulder and elbow.

At that moment Mr. William Wolfskill, one of the remarkable men of the place, and a staunch friend of Colonel Warner, appeared in the doorway of his own business house, and comprehending the status of affairs in the street, advanced toward the crowd, himself well armed. Seeing him and divining his intent, the wounded man cried out:

"Do n't shoot; I do n't want any man killed."

These words had the effect to allay the heat of Espinosa and his company, who, after a short parley, released their captive. Meanwhile the Picos, early informed of the captain's errand, had made their escape. Some days later, however, they, with a half-dozen other prominent citizens, were arrested and conveyed to Santa Barbara "as prisoners of war!" Nearly fifty years have passed away since that day, yet the victim of that rencounter recalls the circumstances as clearly and as readily as if the event had happened only yesterday.

In the year 1846, Colonel Warner secured from the Mexican government a valuable grant of land, embracing twenty-six thousand acres, or six square leagues. The tract adjoined the lands belonging to the San Luis Rey Mission, and also skirted the old through wagon-road from San Diego to Fort Yuma. It lay some sixty miles east of the former place, and one hundred and twenty south-east of Los Angeles. Some time in 1844 Mr. Warner removed his family to this princely estate. Thenceforth it was known as "Warner's Ranch," and bears that name to-day, though years have elapsed since the title thereto was vested in Colonel Warner.

A distinguished Californian, writing upon incidents connected with those dangerous days in this part of the State, says:

"Colonel John J. Warner, a pioneer whose magnificent domain was the first reached by the immigrant after crossing the Colorado desert, was always open-hearted and generous to the wayworn traveler, and nearly impoverished himself by his acts of charitable liberality. All honor to the benevolent old pioneer."

Once in possession of these broad acres, the next step was the stocking them liberally with horses, cattle, and sheep. This Colonel Warner did, and shortly was reputed to be "immensely rich." But to-day, while comfort and plenty find lodgment at the honorable man's fireside, he is no longer a Crœsus of the plains. In some of the many vicissitudes which have swept over this region, probably some of this wealth took wings and flew away. Much of it certainly was expended in charity. Not a little was stolen by marauding Indians, as the following occurrence shows:

The ranchos of that period were kept munificently supplied, not only with groceries and provisions for the entertainment of large companies of guests and frequent needy travelers, but also with a full and often expensive assortment of dry goods. This was especially the case at Colonel Warner's frontier home. The man who could so liberally provide for strangers and friends practiced no parsimony in supplying the wants of his family. One is not surprised that the vast store of necessaries and luxuries always on hand at the Warner rancho should sooner or later excite the cupidity of predatory Indians, of whom a plenty were the colonel's neighbors.

During the year 1851 he was repeatedly warned of a threatened attack from the Cowia tribe, numbering several hundred, and living in villages not far from his estate. Hardly believing the reports, he, however, took the precaution to remove his wife and children to San Diego, starting them out in the night, under escort of one Captain Nye, a sea-faring friend of the family, who happened to be on a visit to the rancho. A little before sunrise the second morning after their departure, the colonel was awakened by the shouts of savages around the house. Having kept watch during the night, he had lain down toward day, taking care not to remove his shoes, and was at the moment in a sound slumber.

On a table at the bedside lay several loaded pistols and a fowling-piece or two. At the rear door stood three saddle horses, tied, and ready for instant mounting. The arms and animals were provided for the escape of himself, his Mexican servant—at that moment being slain by the plunderers, in a corral a few rods away—and a mulatto boy, the servant of an army officer at San Diego. The latter was confined in the house, a helpless victim of rheumatism. He had been sent out from the city to try the water of some notable hot springs on the rancho, and had come over to the house but the day before.

Springing from the bed, Colonel Warner ran, unarmed, to the rear door of the house, and opened it, to ascertain if the horses were yet there. The marauders, about two hundred in number, greeted him with a shower of arrows, not one of which hit him, fortunately.

Stepping quickly to the table, and securing one of the fowling-pieces, he returned to his guests, and found to his dismay that two of the horses had been removed, and that an Indian was in the act of loosing the third. The gun flashed, and the plunderer lay on the ground dead. A second, attempting to take the animal, fell also. Then a third, making the effort, was mortally wounded. Thrown into a panic by these casualties, the band retreated temporarily to a shed near by, bearing the bodies of their fallen comrades.

Resolved now to attempt an escape before the Cowias could rally, and also to save the young invalid in his care, Colonel Warner quickly placed the boy on the horse, put his holster pistols in the saddle, his belt pistols on his person, laid one fowling-piece across the neck of the horse, and suspended another at the animal's side. Then mounting in front of the youth he dashed away, the foe not interfering. On the estate, some miles distant, lay a village of friendly Indians, where were the headquarters of his herdsmen. Thither rode the fugitives with all speed. Immediately thirty trusted Indians were charged with conveying the invalid to St. Isabel, for care and safety, and the herders were dispatched to bring in the stock. Then, accompanied by a number of his own Indian dependents, Colonel Warner hastened back to his home. The Cowias, recovered from their fright, were hurriedly removing from the premises the stock of merchandise, valued at about six thousand dollars. They now showed great hostility, terrifying the man's small escort into a prompt retreat. To oppose the spoilers single-handed, was to meet certain death. The Colonel, therefore, wheeled, rode away and joined his family in San Diego. Upon their return they were attended by a considerable military escort, led by Major, afterwards General, Heinzelman. This rancho, on the verge of the desert, was the home of the family for thirteen years, or until 1857, when Los Angeles once more became their place of residence. The next year witnessed the death of Mrs. Warner.

For Mr. Warner's bravery in saving the life of the colored youth at the risk of his own, he received the title of Colonel—from his friends only, I presume. He was never in the army.

In 1858 Colonel Warner entered journalistic life, as the publisher of the *Southern California Vineyard*, a Democratic sheet, at first devoted to general news, but in time drifting into a strong political paper. But when the Democratic party of California took position in favor of secession, Colonel Warner adhered to the Union, notwithstanding strong party effort to control both him and his paper. As was to be expected, loyalty killed the journal, but failed to kill its editor.

The *Vineyard* breathed its last in 1861. For five years thereafter Colonel Warner was the Southern California correspondent of the *Alta California*.

Previous to becoming a knight of the pen, he served the public in several responsible civil positions. For the sessions of '51 and '52 he represented San Diego County in the Assembly of California; and Los Angeles County in the same body in 1860. He was once elected a judge in San

Diego County, but being long absent in San Francisco never qualified, and never served.

A few years ago Colonel Warner wrote a series of articles on methods for confining the Los Angeles River within its proper channel in seasons of flood. These papers drew attention at the time for their apparent practicability. But with the deceptive stream flowing under ground half the time, and seldom troubling any body very much, his suggestions were not heeded. But the suffering and loss of life and property caused by its overflows last Winter, have led to the republication and serious consideration of these articles.

In the spring of 1884 the aged pioneer completed a lengthy paper on "The Causes of the Cold and Warm Ages in the Arctic Latitudes." His theory, if not correct, is interesting, and reads as follows:

"At one time in the world's history the Continents of North and South America were not as they now are, united by the Isthmus of Panama. All Central America then lay beneath the ocean. Behring's Strait, instead of being a narrow passage of water, was a broad sea, connecting the Pacific and Arctic Oceans. No warm Gulf Stream flowed northward along the eastern coast of North America, and across the Atlantic to the British coast. But an equatorial warm stream of vast proportions flowed from the Atlantic into the Pacific Ocean, over submerged Central America, and on northwestwardly to the north-eastern coast of Asia, where, pouring through Behring's Strait into the Polar Ocean, it converted it into a vast thermal sea, on whose shores flourished a tropical vegetation. Ages passed away, and Behring's Strait became very nearly closed by volcanic upheaval, greatly restricting the flow of warm water into the Northern Ocean. Arctic temperature was the result in those high latitudes. Meanwhile Central America had appeared above the ocean, sending the equatorial warm current northward along the eastern coast of North America, and forming the 'Gulf Stream' of to-day."

In the neighborhood of forty years ago this patriarch paid his first and, up to the present, only visit to his native State. His route was a devious one, taking him from Los Angeles to San Pedro, thence to Acapulco by water, and from there across Mexico to Vera Cruz, whence he went by sail to Mobile, and thence on to the land of steady habits. While in the East he delivered several addresses on California. In the city of Rochester, 1841, he discussed the question of a trans-continental railway, remarking: "Should I ever come East again, I shall come in a railway car." That discussion gives Colonel Warner, instead of Stephen H. Whitney, as has been claimed for him, the honor of being the first man to propose a thoroughfare of steel across the continent of America.

A Los Angeles paper, speaking on this point this morning, says: "Mr. Whitney took up the suggestion and talking upon it, gained much *éclat* in the East for the boldness of the idea, while Colonel Warner, returning to California, lost all credit for it. The honor should certainly be awarded to our esteemed fellow-citizen. It seems to us," the sheet continues, " that the continental railway lines, even at this late day, should deem it an honor to transport, in the most luxurious Pullman car, the venerable gentleman, who, with profound foresight, nearly a half a century ago, first proposed a railway across the American continent."

It may interest the reader to know that the great railways did, in June, after this sketch was written, convey Colonel Warner and the young lady—a grandchild—who attended him, twice across the continent. In an absence of several months in the East, the happy pioneer visited the home of

Chief Justice Waite, in Washington; was received with marked respect by President Arthur, and took a look through all the grand government buildings. Proceeding to New England, he renewed his acquaintance with the scenes and surviving friends of his youth, and, going or returning, passed some time, in a delightful way, among his relatives in and around Cleveland, Ohio; and, as he said to the writer after his return, "was everywhere treated like a prince."

Colonel Warner now resides with a married daughter on Main Street, in Los Angeles, in an old-time adobe home, with its only entrance at the rear of the building. Unfortunately, since making his last eastern trip, he has almost wholly lost his sight. "I can not see you," he said, meeting me on my return to Los Angeles, after an absence of two years, "but I remember your voice." His mental faculties, on the other hand, are perfectly preserved. He was that day serving as a delegate to a county political convention, held in the city. The man is over six feet in height, slender, quite erect. His white hair stands out from his head in all directions. As to the matters of his own life he is modest and reticent, though most of the facts given in this sketch were obtained from his own lips. He is a perfect encyclopedia of information on a host of subjects. He readily recalls the leading events in the history of California for a half-century past, with their exact dates; and also the career of many of its prominent men. He is obliging, at great cost to himself many times. I frequently had occasion, during my residence here, to call upon him for information on some subject. Every time he was the same patient, courteous, self-forgetting gentleman.

## XXI.

## COLONIZATION SCHEMES.

IN no part of the United States, certainly, and, perhaps, nowhere in the world, has the subject of colonization received more earnest and more intelligent consideration than has been given it in Southern California during the past six years. The most enterprising of men have devoted time, strength, ability, and fortunes to devising schemes for settling this part of the coast rapidly and well. There was, the moment the Southern Pacific Road was completed, and still is, ground for pushing and developing this sort of business. Lying on this coast, seven years ago, with a climate nowhere on earth surpassed, was a vast area of country almost literally without house or inhabitant. Of course I know there were villages here, and ranchos, with houses upon them, but that does not weaken the statement I have made. On account of the productiveness of the soil, this area was fitted to become the home of millions of people. Most of it could be given to the plow almost without cutting down a tree or removing a stone, but it was land asleep. During the past week I have ridden over thousands of acres which the implements of husbandry have never touched. Under its covering of thickly blooming flowers—white, pink, blue, purple, and yellow, all tiny but beautiful things—are concealed possibilities of production, so great that I dare not express the facts in the case, lest the reader's incredulity shall break out in words I should not care to hear.

To bring these acres under cultivation, and bring human beings to the enjoyment of their products and the benefits of the delightful climate, as well as to contribute to the resources of the country, while increasing their individual fortunes, are the chief objects sought by the men engaged in the numerous colonization enterprises.

The subject of colonization has at least two sides. It will readily be conceded that all the benefits of the scheme ought not to accrue to the families who settle on colony sites, finding ready to their hand, the moment they arrive on the ground, systems of water, of light, and of education, together with church privileges, a dry-goods store, a grocery, a doctor, a newspaper, and, in many instances, a tasteful new dwelling ready for their occupancy. It is expected, or should be, that the two, ten, or twenty men who purchase a large tract of land in a favorable location; lay it off in lots and parcels; plant upon it trees by the thousand, for shade and fruit; conduct to all parts of it an unfailing supply of pure soft water from some river or mountain spring, miles distant; build a hotel; erect a church and a school-house; secure postal facilities; arrange for telephonic and telegraphic communication with the outside world; work early and late, and hard, to interest people in what they are doing; and lastly, worry until health declines, lest after all, the venture may fail, will reap something of a harvest from the one or two hundred thousand dollars sown in all these improvements.

There are in Southern California a score, probably, of prosperous colonies. Some of them have expanded into beautiful towns and strengthened into extensive fruit-growing communities. In a preceding chapter I have referred to a cluster of such settlements, all lying south-east of Los Angeles, in the Santa Ana Valley. But on the through line of the Southern Pacific Railway, east of the city and within a distance of seventy miles, has been planted another series of such colonies. It will do the reader who has never seen California good to read about them.

Last Thursday afternoon, at four o'clock, the through eastern train on the above road pulled out from the depot in Los Angeles with the writer on board, wound through a dusty street or two, then turned squarely away from the sunset, swept across the nearly dry bed of the Los Angeles River, and struck out for the great Colorado Desert. On our left until long after sunset, the purple Sierra Madres were in full view from the car windows, while short spurs and ranges, named for the whole catalogue of saints, shot out into the plain, over which we were speeding, in every direction. For the first two or three miles out the traveler sees nothing attractive, except a few vineyards and young orange orchards, with occasional residences planted on the hills around.

The first halt is at Alhambra, which suggests Washington Irving and Old Spain, but which consists of little more than a fine hotel, set away on a sightly hill-top under the Sierra Madre. Running on some miles the train stopped in front of the ancient church of the San Gabriel Mission, eleven and a half miles from the city. Here stood this somewhat unique structure when Los Angeles was founded, one hundred years ago. All around it lies the rich and highly cultivated San Gabriel Valley, verdant with all kinds of fruit orchards, and as fragrant with flowers as Ignatius Donnelly claims were the fair plains of the submerged island of Atlantis. It was the floral copy of this church which formed so notable a feature of the San Gabriel exhibit at the brilliant flower festival held in Los Angeles last May.

Next on the list is the incipient town of La Puente, which recalls to mind the fact that the La Puente Rancho in this vicinity, is a tract of land deemed exceedingly rich in petroleum deposit. Some six years ago—1880, I think—two indomitable Canadian gentlemen, the Messrs. George and William Chaffey, founders of the flourishing colony of Ontario, where our train will soon arrive, were engaged, with some others, in developing this source of wealth here. About that time Mr. Burdette Chandler, a gentleman familiar with coal-oil mining in Pennsylvania, began boring for oil on this ranch. At a depth of one hundred and fifty feet he obtained in paying quantities a grade of oil similar to the West Virginia lubricating oil. Three wells were put down to a depth varying from one hundred and fifty to five hundred feet. Each well, produced fifteen barrels per day at the outset. About this time was organized the Chandler Oil Company, for the purpose of developing the petroleum on this ranch. Other wells were then sunk, with flattering results; also a refinery was erected for distilling the oil. In the "Annual Report of the Los Angeles Board of Trade" for 1886, I notice that coal-oil is mentioned as one of the most promising resources of Los Angeles County. It is well known that the county abounds with oil springs, asphaltum beds, and mines of brea.

The celebrated Brea Rancho, situated some eight or nine miles north-west of Los Angeles, affords a splendid example of the bituminous deposit of the region. Originally this was a large and valuable estate, whose proprietor, becoming pecuniarily involved, mortgaged portions of it to enable him to meet his obligations. But before the debts were liquidated death released him from his burdens, transferring them to the shoulders of his widow. She bravely faced the responsibility, sold enough of the estate to cancel the mortgages, and then began mining the brea as a source of income for herself, reducing it on the estate, to a form convenient for making cement pavement for streets. The whole was a piece of good management, and the lady now finds herself on the road to independence. Five hundred acres of this property are the possession of ex-Senator Cornelius Cole, of California, appointed some years ago to settle the claims of the Pacific Coast creditors in the notorious Alabama case.

But while we have been talking about coal-oil the train has run on to Pomona, an enterprising village thirty-three miles from the city, and the spot, of all others in Southern California, on which the Goddess of Fruits should shower her favors, since it bears her name. The place has existed but a few years, and has a population of twenty-five hundred people probably. Being a part of the great plain which slopes southward from the base of the Sierra Madre, its soil is inexhaustibly fertile, and its climate almost faultless. Groves of semi-tropical fruits flourish on all sides. A perennial supply of pure water is furnished by a stream which breaks from the mountains back of it. That the place has schools, churches, and other facilities for the improvement of the citizens, goes without saying. For years to come, Pomona will be associated with the name of that admirable Christian man, Rev. C. T. Mills, who, with his capable wife, founded Mills Seminary near Oakland, California, a number of years ago. At one time Dr. Mills represented a large interest in the land on which this village stands, and his wise assistance in the development of the colony insured the gratifying progress we now see. While here attending to its interests, one day, he met with the accident that cost him his life. Being thrown from his carriage, he received an injury to one of his arms which resulted in amputation, and subsequently in death. Thus was Mrs. Mills, assisted by a board of trustees, left the sole head of the institution, and also an important member of the Pomona Land Company. Dr. Mills, who was for some years president of Batticotta Theological Seminary, India, and also of Oahu College for Young Men in Honolulu, had the respect and friendship of many prominent people in this country.

Four miles further eastward, the train halts in front of the trim little station-house at Ontario. The tasteful building, with its surrounding of gay flowers and borderings of bright color, looks more like a summer-house on some gentleman's estate, than like a temporary shelter for passengers, and the business office of the railway. The place takes its name from Ontario, Canada, where its founders, the Chaffey brothers, spent their youth. Their father was once the owner of large shipping interests in the old Canadian city, and established quite a commerce with certain American towns. As the train draws up, passengers on the village side of the cars exclaim: "What a pretty place!" But I happen to know that a little over four years ago not one building, and but a single tree, relieved the thousand desolate acres now changed into this pleasant scene. Less than three years since, I visited the place for the purpose of studying the practical workings of colonization schemes. The town was then undergoing wide advertising as "the model colony" of Southern California, and was a place of great interest for many reasons, but the reader will be most concerned in its present situation.

Ontario lies in San Bernardino County, the largest county in the State (having an area of ten million acres), is thirty-eight miles east of Los Angeles, and is a part of the territory known as the "warm belt," a strip of country from eight to ten miles wide, which skirts, for a distance of seventy miles, from west to east, the base of the Sierra Madre Mountains, and includes all the thriving towns between Pasadena and the San Gorgonio Pass. This district is seldom visited by frosts, never by severe ones. It may be irrigated in every part by water from the rivers which traverse it from north to south, or from mountain springs and torrents. It is therefore admirably adapted to the culture of both northern and semi-tropical fruits.

Ontario may also be said to lie in what is termed the Upper Santa Ana Valley, between two lofty ranges of mountains, the Sierra Madre, ten miles away on the north, the Temescal, fifteen miles distant on the south. In every direction the view from the place is very fine. The town plat is a part of a tract of ten thousand acres to be devoted to the colony. Purer air can nowhere be breathed. Through the center of the tract, from the railway to the nearer mountains, stretches a beautiful avenue, seven miles long, two hundred feet wide, as straight as surveyor's chain could make it, with an ascending grade toward the Sierra of one thousand feet. Through the middle of this avenue was originally allotted a space forty feet wide for a double line of cable railway to be operated by water. But as the cars stopped opposite the magnificent thoroughfare, a passenger remarked:

"The Ontario Land Company is about to lay the rails for an electric road up one of those drives to the mountains, and thence around to the mouth of the famous San Antonio cañon."

Planted on both sides of this forty feet is a row of fan palms, alternating with the eucalyptus, or the pepper tree. Both the latter are rapid growers, and are set to secure temporary shade and tree effects until the palms make a display, when they will be removed. The imposing effect of this double row of the fan palm, when sufficiently grown, must be seen to be appreciated. Again, on either side of this central way, extends a carriage drive, sixty-five feet wide, very smooth, never dusty, and lined, next the sidewalk, by a row of grevillia and pepper trees, with the eucalyptus interspersed. The grevillia is a handsome tree, evergreen, with bushy, spreading crown, and general appearance like that of the pepper tree, over which, however, it has the advantage of preserving a smooth, clean trunk in old age. Finally, fifteen feet are reserved on both sides this avenue for sidewalks and external parks of flowers. Many of the lots fronting upon this street have been fenced with a hedge of the Monterey cypress. Should this hedge be continued to the mountains, there will appear two low, trim lines of vivid green, seven miles long, doing away with unpicturesque fencings of wood and iron. Now imagine this broad roadway embellished with six rows of varied and fadeless green, the whole flanked with a wealth of beautiful bloom. Think of a drive at early morning, or after tea, up this smooth ascent, with the Sierra rising right before one and a health-giving breeze fanning the cheek. I myself rode over it when all this charm of vegetation was at the starting point, before the grade was established quite to the mountains. It was a delightful ride. But with all this ornamentation at maturity, there will be not another such street in California, unless a rival be found in Magnolia Avenue, at Riverside, of which we shall have a word to say further on; nor on the continent, except it be Euclid Avenue, in Cleveland, Ohio, whose name it borrows. The Ontario Euclid embraces one hundred and eighty acres of land, and is adorned with something like seventy thousand trees, and is twice the width of Cleveland's beautiful street.

At the time of my first visit, eighteen months after the ground was broken, seventy families were settled upon the tract; a public school was in progress; postal and telegraph facilities had been secured; a commodious hotel had been erected, and the varied work of laying off lots, grading streets, putting down water-pipes, tunneling the mountains for unfailing water, setting vines for raisins, and planting a great variety of fruit trees, was going on with a will, besides building for this purpose and for that. Two years have passed since that day, changing the scene wondrously. How so much could have been done in so little time is a marvel.

The soil of this warm belt is a sandy, gravelly loam, lying gently inclined to the southern and western sun, and is easily worked. Dense fogs, a serious hindrance in some localities to the curing of raisins, are said to visit Ontario too seldom to be taken into account.

It should now be said that the interests of the colony have passed from the hands of its founders. Some months ago a gentleman representing an Australian colonization company arrived in Los Angeles for the purpose of investigating the colonization schemes of Southern California. The fame of Ontario had reached his ears. He paid the place a visit. The plan of these brothers commended itself to his judgment. He conferred with them as to the feasibility of undertaking a similar enterprise on land near the city of Melbourne. The result was a proposition to the Messrs. Chaffey to transplant a colony of English people from the mother country to the Fifth Continent. Mr. George Chaffey soon sailed for Australia to look the field over. A grant of twenty-five thousand acres of land was offered him for the project. He accepted it, and decided to sell his interests in Ontario and remove his family to Melbourne. Returning to America he soon accomplished these steps, and is now domiciled in the far-off land with his wife and children. Mr. William Chaffey and his family, it is understood, follow at a later day. This gentleman is also known as having been active a few years earlier in adorning that section of the town of Riverside called Arlington. These young men seem to possess a genius for taking the virgin soil and building up towns upon it. Their success at both Ontario and Etiwanda, Mr. George Chaffey's place of residence, is strong evidence to that effect. I have it from a personal friend of this man, that when he arrived in Los Angeles, less than five years ago, "the sum of his wealth was four dollars." If that be true, Ontario, made to spring out of the naked mesa in the space of four years, with all its present beauty, homes, and business, proves what wonders can be accomplished by sheer courage, energy, and industry, linked with a taste for education, and a reverence for God and religion.

A feature of special importance at Ontario is the noble San Antonio cañon. From the head of Euclid Avenue a carriage road winds off to the left, among the few low foot-hills of the Sierra Madre. After several hundred rods of distance, it turns and enters the rock-strown mouth of this grand gorge, penetrating the Sierra not less than nine miles. Down this wild passage flows the clear, cold, roaring, tumbling stream, which gives the colony its splendid drinking water. Speckled trout abound in it, as do quail among the foot-hills and loftier heights, making the place a paradise for the angler and the hunter. But the place has higher recommendations than its fine scenery and myriad life in air and water. It is an Eden for sufferers from asthma and rheumatism. Relief from these troubles has been, almost immediate in some cases, at the entrance to this cañon. A well-known physician of Chicago relates that a severe case of asthma was greatly mitigated after one hour spent here, and a trying case of sciatic rheumatism yielded after a a two weeks' sojourn.

In a tent pitched on a grassy plot, among some trees, at the opening to this gorge, there lived in 1884 a gentleman from San Francisco, who had long been afflicted with asthma of a terrible type. So long as he remained in the cañon his enemy let him alone, but the moment he ventured into Los Angeles for twenty-four hours, the disease attacked him so fiercely that he was glad to hasten back to his retreat under the shadow of the everlasting hills. He pronounces the spot the best for his malady he has ever found.

Nor is the resort without attractions for well people. Numbers visit the locality every year for refreshment. Business men jaded with care and anxiety find new strength beside its merry stream. Romping among the granite bowlders, pining children become hardy as little bears. And such an appetite as people get! The most provident cook would be taxed to meet its demands. Some three years ago Mr. William Chaffey, worn with the burden of Ontario affairs, removed his wife and children to the canon and camped for several weeks. Speaking of that time, he told me that when ready to return to his home he felt strong enough to found another colony. A fair road extends up the deep rent in the mountains for a distance of some miles. Mount Baldy, the regal, snow-capped summit mentioned in an early chapter of this book, stands at its head, eight miles from the mouth, and sixteen from Ontario and the Southern Pacific road. The monarch is worthy a visit. Its height is nine thousand feet.

In all this ten thousand acres of inclined plane there is not an acre of marsh or fen; not a rod over which malaria dare hover; scarcely a foot which the health-giving sunshine does not bless. A thick fog rarely finds its way this distance from the sea. Sometimes a thin vapor floats over the tract just before morning, but even that vanishes soon after breakfast. About two o'clock, as sure as the afternoon comes, a refreshing breeze springs up and continues until sunset. The average temperature of the Summer days is eighty degrees. The evenings are cool. Warm wraps are then necessary.

## XXII.

## VINEYARDS AND ORANGE GROVES.

IN Southern California all distances are measured from Los Angeles. I mention, therefore, that Riverside, with its beautiful suburb, Arlington—I am not sure but that I should say Arlington, with its less attractive suburb, Riverside—is located sixty-eight miles south-east of that city, and seven miles south of the Southern Pacific Railway. I entered the place in an open, high-seated, square-topped "stage," having left the train at Colton, nine miles distant. The vehicle tossed its load of six passengers about in a merciless fashion, but afforded us a fine view of the hills and valleys at every turn. Along most of our course wild flowers covered the ground as with a carpet. There were millions upon millions of the tiny things, exquisite in coloring, dainty in shape.

Every feature and aspect of Riverside is rural. A day's ride through the State of Ohio by rail, in any direction, would reveal twenty such villages, omitting the vineyards, orange groves, cypress hedges, eucalypti, and fan palms of Riverside.

"That sounds like omitting a great deal," says the reader. It is.

The whole vicinity of Riverside and Arlington furnishes indubitable evidence that somebody works in the valley. Yet during a drive of eight miles yesterday afternoon past an almost unbroken succession of orange groves and vineyards, I actually saw only three men engaged in their cultivation. The grounds and trees were faultlessly clean. The leaves of the orange trees looked as if they had been subjected to an application of polishing powder, so glossy and bright were they. Probably the secret of all this tidiness, was, that the golden fruit had been gathered by the shippers, and any trimming the trees required after that, had been done and the ground carefully raked. The vines likewise had had their pruning and were growing finely. Thus was the Spring work of the horticulturists "done up," just as housekeepers do up their Spring cleaning. The extreme neatness of some of the orchards added immensely to their attractions. I had visited fine orange orchards in Florida, but never had I seen a sight to compare with these miles upon miles of glistening trees. From the road to far back in the distance stretched the diagonal rows as straight as hand of man could set them.

To have stopped a few moments here and there, simply to look at them, would have been a satisfaction, but I was taking a hurried drive and could not tarry.

In 1884 Riverside had the largest acreage of vines and trees of any of the colonies giving attention to orange and raisin culture south of the Sierra Madre. Yet no farther back than 1870, this valley, now so smiling and yielding such lavish returns to its cultivators, was but a silent waste, mantled in Spring-time with gay flowers and tall wild grasses. The soil is composed largely of disintegrated rock, washed from the surrounding mountains by the storms of ages, and possesses almost boundless powers of production. But these powers were dormant. Something was needed to arouse them, and that something was simply the voice of running water. The making this discovery has changed the face of Nature all over this section of our country. There was more sense in General Fremont's idea of flooding the Colorado Desert, or portions of it, in order to render it productive, than he has ever had credit for. He has been laughed at for his supposed *want* of sense in even thinking of so shallow a project. Yet experiment has proved that water is the one thing necessary to convert miles of those arid stretches into fruitful gardens.

In September of 1870 the Southern California Colony Association was formed for the purpose of buying and selling lands, and of appropriating the water of the Santa Ana River to the irrigation of sixteen townships. The next year, in June, a canal was finished to the hamlet now called Riverside. Then began the experiments in irrigation. Wonderful mutation! Then, the barren land. To-day, fruit, bloom, and beauty everywhere, with fortunes making and fortunes promised, all out of the once somnolent soil.

In the chapter on Ontario reference was made to Magnolia Avenue, in Arlington, which is but an extension of Riverside, and contains many pretty streets and handsome homes, Riverside being the business portion of the place. It includes the hotels, stores, newspaper offices, and all kinds of shops. But Arlington's street, *par excellence*, is Magnolia Avenue, consisting of a double driveway, each lined on both sides by a row of pepper, eucalyptus, fan-palm, and grevillia trees, alternating in places. The appearance of the street is magnificent. The effect is produced mainly by the two passageways and the several lines of trees, intensified by the presence of the palms, and by plats of brilliant flowers blooming between the curb-stone and sidewalk in front of some of the residences. Merely as a street Magnolia Avenue far transcends the world-renowned Euclid Avenue in Cleveland. But the moment the lawns and residences of Euclid Avenue are placed in the picture, it completely eclipses the Arlington thoroughfare. There are some fine dwellings, however, among these orange groves, themselves a feature which can never grace the Cleveland street.

In orange culture Riverside is supposed to rival the best orange-fields of the continent. Eminent among the varieties grown here is the Riverside Naval, an orange of Brazilian origin, and surpassing in size and flavor, as some think, the luscious Indian River orange of Florida. At the California fruit exhibits it has "often taken the premium over all competitors," being pronounced the best orange grown in the United States. About 1885 a blood orange, in flavor superior to the well-known Malta, made its appearance in this valley, coming from the Island of Tahiti. There are said to be growing in Southern California thirty-three varieties of oranges, and fourteen or more kinds of lemons.

### RAISIN CULTURE AT RIVERSIDE.

But it is as a center of raisin culture, perhaps, that Riverside comes most prominently to the front among the colonies of Southern California. I should say, without the figures at hand to prove it, that its shipments of this fruit exceed those from all other points combined. In this valley much study and intelligent experiment have been given to the industry, and it has been learned that four conditions are indispensable to success in the pursuit. These are: A rich, warm, well-drained soil; a dry atmosphere; skillful cultivation of the soil, and a high temperature for curing the fruit. All these requisites seem to obtain at Riverside. The reader may have supposed that raisins can be made wherever grapes can be grown. A few observations taken in a raisin-making community would banish that notion. Grapes can be grown where rains are frequent; but a shower when raisins are curing, is an undesirable visitor. The details of the industry are very interesting. If the reader will peruse the following paragraphs he will get a good idea of how raisins are made. Most of the information given was derived from the Messrs. Orrin and William Backus, intelligent raisin-growers at Riverside.

The grape most in favor with the Riverside culturists, and the one from which their best raisins are made, is the Muscat of Alexandria, a native of Northern Africa. Besides this, there are much cultivated, the Muscatel Gordo Blanco, a large, white, pulpy grape, of high flavor; and the Seedless Sultana, a small, white, prolific variety, mainly used for cooking. The Muscat, however, is the staple grape for raisins. Under favorable circumstances it yields very large, open clusters, which, when ripe, are of a light, amber color, firm in flesh and rich in sugar. The seeds are small, and the flavor very fine. The Muscat vine is peculiarly sensitive to cold and dampness, especially at the period of inflorescence. Such a state of weather is quite certain to produce sterile blossoms. It is for this reason that the Muscat is not so well adapted to the northern part of the State, where showers and heavy fogs are frequent. Also, the occurrence of a few extremely hot days in Summer will cause the berries to fall; while a chilly season delays their maturing, and increases the labor of curing them.

A raisin vineyard is in full bearing at eight years from the planting. Properly cared for after that age, it ought to yield bountifully for at least forty years. Some of the vineyards of the Mission Grape—a wine-making fruit—planted in California by the Franciscan Fathers, are a century old, yet but a few years since, the black, distorted stumps of one of these vineyards were to be seen fruiting in the neighborhood of Aliso Street, in Los Angeles. Once in bearing, therefore, a raisin vineyard may be a source of income during the owner's life-time; and, should he be early removed by death, is a desirable property to leave his family.

The operations of pruning and irrigating the vines; of picking, drying, and packing the raisins, require the exercise of skill and intelligence, if the vineyardist would reap a harvest from his investment. In the singular soil of California nature has hidden away many a fortune, and if man would persuade her to unlock them for his benefit, he must work in harmony with her plans. Therefore, if she requires grapevines to be trimmed down to two eyes, instead of more, his wisest course is to obey her. If she resents having the soil washed away from, rather than properly soaked above their roots, during irrigation, he had better gracefully yield the point. Prodigal irrigation meets its punishment in deteriorated fruits and impoverished fields. How often and how much to irrigate, are important questions in California. Location, the character of the soil, and the variation in the seasons, modify the answer. The fruit-grower must use his judgment, and his experience, in deciding the case.

In planting vines for raisins, cuttings from eighteen to twenty inches in length, and bearing from three to five healthy buds, are preferred. The cutting is made close to one bud, and that one, with one or two others, is buried firmly beneath the well-prepared soil.

The customary, and probably best time for pruning is in December and January. It may be done at any time after the leaves fall and before the buds start. A second or "Summer pruning" is practiced by some vine-dressers. But the step is objected to by others, on the ground that removing many of the leaves exposes the berries to sun-burn. At the Winter pruning Mr. Backus, who has made an earnest study of the soil and climate, cuts his canes down to ten or twelve inches from the ground. It is considered that a low, strong stump, with short spurs for the fruit, insures better results than does a greater length of vine. Just before the buds start, the ground is plowed and irrigated thoroughly. If a second and later irrigation can be avoided, the better. If not, just enough water should be given the vines to ripen the fruit. To insure first-class raisins, the grapes must be fully ripe when cut.

When the Muscat berries have taken on a clear, bright, amber color, as they do between the first and middle of September, they are ready for the picking. Chinese and Indians are usually employed for this branch of the work. In some vineyards the picking is done by the day, in others by the tray, the wages varying from $1.50 to $2.00 per day. Each picker removes the clusters from two rows of vines at the same time, placing them on wooden trays capable of holding twenty pounds each, which are placed at intervals between the rows. In the picking great care is taken not to remove the "bloom" from the fruit with the hands, as that detracts from the appearance of the raisins. Three trays, of twenty pounds each, will make twenty pounds of raisins. Thus the fruit shrinks about two-thirds in curing.

The weather being favorable, the raisins will dry in about fourteen days. Should a shower fall while they are curing, the trays must be "stacked," several in a company, the sides being well protected in some way. By this arrangement the berries will stand a heavy rain without injury. It has been learned that to *incline* the trays to the sun on favorable days hastens the drying. The fruit is turned but once during the fourteen days, but the act requires some dexterity, as a tray-full is turned by a single movement. It is accomplished by inverting an empty tray upon a full one, and turning both simultaneously, the full tray thus becomes the empty one. Two men are required for the deed.

By some parties the trays are allowed to remain on the ground between the rows during the drying. By others they are disposed in an open space, where the fruit may have the full fervor of the sun and the free sweep of the air. Formerly it was the custom to lay the clusters on the bare ground to dry, and to turn each one by hand. Laying them on paper superseded this practice. Boards were next adopted. Then followed frames made of lath. Trays are the latest invention.

The berries not being uniform in size, there results unevenness in the curing. Before they are packed, however, not only must the moisture be equalized, but the aroma must be developed; also the fragile stems must be rendered pliable, else the clusters will be broken in the packing. All these results are secured by placing the trays in contrivances called "sweat-boxes" for a few days. Here the fruit is "evened up," or brought to the requisite condition for the final step. On removal from the sweat-box the bunches are assorted into Layers, London Layers, and Loose Muscatels. From this last grade the Riverside Packing Company selects the small seedless raisins and rates them as "Seedless Sultanas," though not one of them is the fruit of a Sultana vine. Some parties cull from the trays, before the turning, such stems as will rank as London Layers, and place them on separate trays, where they may dry uniformly.

After the distribution into classes, the raisins are weighed into parcels of five pounds each. The packer then presses each package into close shape, places it in a mold of proper size, puts that under a lever-press until the fruit is quite compact, when he drops it, wrapped in fine white paper, into the box in which it is to go to market. Raisin-boxes are graded in sizes to hold two-and-a-half, five, ten, and twenty pounds each. The last are known as whole boxes, and always contain four of the five-pound packages.

The yield of raisins from the vicinity of Riverside is very great. In 1883 it amounted to sixty thousand boxes. At that time most of the vineyards had about half reached maturity. Thirty-three tons per acre, or two thousand two hundred and thirty trays, each averaging twenty pounds, was the product of Mr. Backus's young vineyard that year. Of course, the harvest has vastly increased since that time.

California raisin-makers have learned that vines permitted to overbear, produce an inferior quality of fruit, a much finer flavor being obtained when prodigality of production is checked. It is said that, for a prime quality of raisins, the Malaga grower, who received the award for the best raisins shown at the Philadelphia Centennial, allows his vines to produce only two pounds of fruit each.

## XXIII.

## THE PICOS AND THE SURRENDER OF CAHUENGA.

IMMEDIATELY after my return from my jaunt to Riverside, I met at her pleasant home, near the First Presbyterian Church, in Los Angeles, a daughter of General Andrez Pico, the Mexican officer who surrendered to Captain, now General J. C. Fremont, in 1848, if I am correct—I write from memory as to the date—the famous Cahuenga Pass, a rudely fortified position some nine miles from the city, in the San Fernando Mountains. This event in the history of Southern California is one of which a stranger in this part of the State often hears. And it is not an infrequent thing for such to be asked:

"Have you visited the Cahuenga Pass yet?"

Having answered my share of such interrogatories in the negative, and hoping to obtain from this daughter a correct version of the action at Cahuenga, I called at her home. The lady, loyal to the Pico blood in her veins, was affable in manner, and appeared interested in my errand.

She had "often heard the story—the Mexican side of it—but, unfortunately, her memory was not reliable; and, besides, Mexican women were not accustomed to remember those matters as the American women do." Then she urged me to "see her uncle, Don Pio Pico, at his residence in the old quarter of the city," or to call "upon Colonel Warner, a life-long friend of Don Pio. Either of those gentlemen could tell exactly how Cahuenga was delivered up to the Americans by her father."

So wending my way through High Street, until I came to a long, low, adobe house, standing back some little distance from the corner of Castellar Street, in that part of the city called Sonoratown, I inquired of a Mexican woman in the yard if the place were the residence of Don Pio Pico.

"It is," she replied, "but he is not here. He is at Ranchita, his country home, a few miles out of the city, and comes in to-morrow. But walk in, and I will find the Señora Ortega, the sister of Don Pio, who will be glad to see you, although she speaks little English."

While the woman kindly sought the Señora, who was employed in the domestic apartments of the house, I took note of the surroundings. The house stands in an ample yard, fenced with boards, at the base of the high hill which terminates Fort Street, near Temple. A long piazza finishes the eastern side. Upon this open the five or six rooms, all on the ground-floor, which compose the dwelling. Externally and internally it is far from palatial. The apartment which serves as a family sitting-room and parlor for guests, is innocent of carpet, except that a short strip of tapestry Brussels answers the purpose of a rug in front of the sofa. A couple of small stands, a willow chair or two, and a set of furniture upholstered in green reps, faded and worn, with the wood-work stained to imitate rosewood, render the place home-like, a variety of bright ornaments and fixtures on the white wall adding to this effect. Every thing was in perfect order, and the house scrupulously clean throughout, showing that Mrs. Ortega is a good housekeeper.

Presently in came the lady, small, homely, wrinkled, aged seventy-four, ignorant of English, but very courteous and quick to understand. From a niece who accompanied her—the Mrs. Perkins, of Santa Barbara, of whom I have already spoken— I learned that Mrs. Ortega is one of a family of eleven children, of whom eight were daughters, and of whom only three survive, herself, a sister in

Santa Barbara, aged eighty-eight, and Don Pio Pico, now eighty-four, each one being remarkably active and hale. The Picos are native Californians, but of true Spanish descent, and in intellectual qualities surpass the average of the race.

The father of the family was a corporal in the Spanish army. At the beginning of this century he was stationed at the well-known Mission of San Gabriel, where he died many years ago. His eldest son, Jose Antonio Pico, was an officer in the Mexican army, from his early manhood until the accession of California, and reached the grade of lieutenant.

The youngest son, Andrez Pico, was also an officer in that army, and attained the rank of general. It was he who figured as the Mexican commander in a sharp conflict with a force of American infantry, under one Captain Gray, at San Pasqual, in December, 1846, and soon afterwards, in conducting the negotiations preliminary thereto, and concluding the famous treaty of Cahuenga, with Captain Fremont. On the part of the Mexican leader, the last affair was a brilliant achievement, in which, according to some authorities, he completely outgeneraled the American officer. The substance of a graphic account of the event, as contained in the "Reminiscences of a Ranger," by Major Horace Bell, is here appended:

"As Colonel Fremont approached Cahuenga, frowning artillery confronting him from the intrenchments, he was met with a flag of truce from General Pico within the stronghold. A parley ensued, and the treaty of Cahuenga was the result. Representing the Republic of Mexico, Pico proposed to disband his force, the officers retaining their private arms; to deliver to Captain Fremont all the arms and munitions of war at the Pass, and to permit the latter to march, without opposition, into the city of Los Angeles, on condition that he— General Pico—should have two hours in which to make his preparations and retire his force from the fort, after which the American commander might march in and take possession.

"On his part Colonel Fremont agreed that the Mexican force should be allowed to retire peaceably to their homes, and there remain unmolested; and also that certain Mexican officers who had violated their paroles in the preceding September, should be pardoned. Having affixed their signatures to the treaty, each commander retaining a copy, General Pico, at the head of about forty men, withdrew from the fort, and the Americans marched in.

"The spoils, which by this treaty passed out of the hands of humbled Mexico, were two batteries of artillery, consisting of a dozen live-oak logs, mounted on as many native corretas; one venerable blunderbuss, the date of which, engraved upon it, suggested service at the siege of Granada; two flint-lock Spanish holster-pistols, and forty Mexican ox-goads, with gay pennons attached."

Don Andreas Pico is said to have been a great humorist, and to have taken much delight in laughing over his Quaker demonstrations at Cahuenga. During the governorship of General Micheltoreno over California, General Pico was his aid-de-camp. After the acquirement of the province by the United States, he held several responsible positions under both the State and general governments. And subsequent to the admission of California into the Union, he represented the county of Los Angeles in the State General Assembly, and the Southern District of California in the Senate. He was a man who had many friends. His demise occurred some nine years ago.

The surviving brother, Don Pio Pico, seems not to have had a taste for military life; or if so, the circumstances of his youth precluded his entering the Mexican army. He however became prominent in the political changes which took place in California, from about the year 1831 onward to 1846. From a warm personal friend of the gentleman, I have the following facts in his career:

In his youth he had but narrow opportunities for education. He however learned to read and write well in Spanish, and acquired a good knowledge of arithmetic. In early manhood, his father having died, he was left without patrimony, to provide for his widowed mother and several sisters. But he proved himself an admirable manager, and accumulated property until, at the age of forty-five, he had the reputation throughout Southern California of being a wealthy man. At that period, 1845, himself and his brother Andrez were joint proprietors of the magnificent rancho of Santa Margarita, in San Diego County. The property comprised ninety thousand acres. There roamed upon it from six to eight thousand head of cattle, common property also.

In addition to this Don Pio Pico was the sole owner of a valuable estate situated in Los Angeles County, some twelve or fourteen miles from the city, and called Ranchita. This he still retains, spending most of his time upon it. Subsequently he acquired considerable property in Los Angeles, the site on which the "Pico House" now stands, and that building itself, being a part of it.

In 1834, Mr. Pico, having become attached to a young Spanish woman by the name of Maria Ignacia Alvarado, entered the matrimonial state. The lady was a distinguished beauty, and a person of fascinating manners. Speaking of her yesterday, a Spanish woman who knew her well said to me:

"You should have seen her. Words can not express her looks, nor her charming ways when she conversed with people. She smiled the most sweetly of all women."

Twenty-four years have passed away since this lovely woman died, leaving no children. Tenderly cherishing her memory, Governor Pico has never married again. At that time it was quite the custom among Mexican women, as it now is, to smoke cigarettes. Mrs. Pico is said to have indulged in this practice occasionally. But her husband carried the habit to excess, being an almost constant smoker. The friend I am quoting in this particular states that one day during the lady's final illness, herself and Don Pio were enjoying their cigarettes together, when she was seized with a terrible rigor, which terminated in death in about an hour. "From that day to the present," said my informant, "Don Pio Pico has never smoked."

Upon the expulsion of Governor Micheltoreno, as the executive of California, in 1839, I think, Mr. Pico, by virtue of being the senior member of the California Legislature, became ex-officio governor of the province. Afterward he was elected and appointed "Governor of the Department of the Californias," as provided under the Constitution of Mexico. This position he retained until the transfer of what is now the State of California to the United States, August 14, 1846. During his administration the city of Los Angeles was the seat of government. Just preceding its occupation by the American forces, Governor Pico judged it prudent, for political reasons, to withdraw from his capital. Retiring to Lower California, he crossed thence to the State of Sonora, where he remained in exile until some time in '49 or '50, since which time he has resided in or near this city.

At the secularization of the California Missions by the Mexican Government, Don Pio Pico was appointed administrator of the Mission of San Luis Rey, an important position, and one he maintained for a number of years. About the same time General Andrez Pico was made one of the grantees of the magnificent estate belonging to the Mission of San Fernando, lying in the fertile valley of that name. The interest in this property also was held in common by the two brothers. After a time Don Pio acquired his brother's claim and eventually sold it for a large sum of money.

For years past the Catholic Church has been at law for the recovery of both these princely domains, and yesterday morning a Catholic priest informed me, with a somewhat triumphant air, that the Church had succeeded, the San Fernando property having recently fallen into her hands.

Don Pio, "the last of the Picos," is a person who, once seen, could not well be forgotten. He is of medium height, stoutly built, with straight shoulders, full face, dark eyes, snowy hair, and brown skin. He is social, charitable, polished in manners. These gifts and graces win him the high regard of all acquaintances, and the admiration of his kindred. He is one of the few representatives remaining of the Mexican *régime* in California.

## XXIV.

## TIME BEGUILES YOU.

A SINGULAR feature of life in Southern California is the apparent rapid flight of time. The days seem to come and go on the wings of the wind. A very short sojourn on the coast suffices to produce this impression. Nor is it made only upon the strangers who tarry but for a Winter, or a year. Even old residents of the country say there is something remarkable in the haste with which the passing part of eternity speeds by.

"Here Time waits for nobody, I assure you," said a citizen lately, who had enjoyed the Pacific breeze for twelve years. "I used to wonder if this impression, of no length to the days, would not wear off after a while; but I see no difference. Slow time must have gone out with the dreaming Mexicans."

Said a lady from Chicago to the writer a few days since: "What an alarming hurry the days are in on this strange coast! It is noon before sunrise, and night before midday. I have the feeling all the while, that I must in some way chain the time until I can accomplish something."

My own experience confirms these statements. Eight months have elapsed since my entrance into this old Spanish town, yet, should I be informed that half that number is the real length of time, I should accept the announcement as correct. Even young persons, for whom Father Time, accoutered with hour-glass and scythe, is usually much too slow, appear to be quite satisfied with the progress the quaint old fellow makes in the Golden State.

How to account for this influence is difficult. There seems to exist in the country a something which cheats the senses. Whether it be in the air, the sunshine, in the ocean breeze, or in all these combined, I can not say. Certainly the climate is not the home-made, common-sense article of the ante-Rocky Mountain States. It is a product of consummate art. There is a variety in the evenness of the weather, and a strange evenness in this variety, which throws an unreality around life, and not more, so far as I can learn, in the case of persons especially affected by climatic influences than of those whose feelings do not rise and fall with the thermometer. All alike walk and work in a dream. Something beguiles, deludes, plays falsely with the senses. Were only the aged, or the ill, or the sorrowful, subjects of the influence, the matter would be less worthy of remark. But since old and young, sad and happy, are its victims, there is some ground for the attention I am giving the subject.

It appears to make trifling difference in the case how closely one applies one's self. The effect is the same. I seat myself to write at nine o'clock in the morning. In an incredibly short time it is one o'clock. I realize that I am hungry. I take my light dinner of bread and peaches, and return to my task. Ere I am aware the sun is dropping into the Pacific. I find myself unspeakably tired, but have had no appreciation of the passage of the day. Had I been at home, on the southern shore of much maligned Lake Erie, I should have "sensed" the going by of nine honest, substantial hours, though I had been just as busy. Now, I am not finding fault with this state of things. I rather like it. I think all the people do. It is in keeping with every thing else on this coast. Every thing is new and peculiar and wonderful.

A friend under this roof says she has "dreamed away eleven years in this city, since bidding adieu to the rigor of Michigan Winters," and, so far as her "realizing its length is concerned, the time might as well have been two years as eleven." She declares that frequently upon awakening in the morning, she has to ask herself what day of the week it is, and sometimes what season of the year, so uncertain is she as to just where the time is. This suggests that indefinite ideas of the days and seasons are due, certainly in part, to the slight change which marks the seasons. Scores upon scores of days are alike as to warmth, brightness, and beauty. Flowers bloom the year round. Most of the trees wear a changeless dress.

### DO THEY NEVER SLEEP?

Another strange characteristic of the country is the sleeplessness of the fowls and dogs. I can not remember to have wakened once in the night since my advent into Los Angeles, when a multitude of these creatures were not doing their "level best" to excel in exercising their vocal organs. The result, of course, is an intense and wide-spread din, a great volume of crowings and barkings. The air is filled with the music, and sleep is driven to the mountains, or out to sea.

However, in this respect California can not hold a candle—excuse the expression—to old-new Arizona. During a week spent in the unique but interesting city of Tucson last Winter, a small colony of fowls was "corraled" in the court of the house in which I lodged. A window of my room, which I was obliged to have open at night for fresh air, opened upon this court. Those feathered people must have understood that I was a stranger in the land of silver and gold, and have desired to give me a cordial welcome, for every night, presumably at great cost of comfort to themselves, they arranged an all-night concert for my entertainment. Several neighboring companies joined heartily in the choruses, and with such force as to convince me that the domestic bird of Arizona excels the world in vocal talent. I can account for the steady nightly music of the Los Angeles fowls, on the ground that the city is so well lighted that they can not distinguish night from day, but why those of Arizona should never sleep is a mystery.

### A THUNDER SHOWER IN MIDSUMMER.

About mid-afternoon yesterday, several unusual sounds caused the citizens to step quickly to the doors and take a look at the sky. These rare noises were simply a few moderate peals of thunder. It being Sunday, most of the week-day clamor was hushed. Thus were the tones from the heavens all the more distinct and startling. Not more surprised, though undoubtedly more alarmed, would the people have been had the notes been the premonitions of an earthquake. A sensible daughter in the household, looking up from her book, said:

"Well, we have lived in this city eleven years, and this is the first time I have heard thunder in Summer. We occasionally, in Winter, hear such reminders of our Michigan home, but never after April." It was then the 4th of August.

A lady residing in San Bernardino affirms that it was the first time she had listened to such music in midsummer, during a sojourn of thirteen years in Southern California. These remarks attest the rarity of electrical phenomena on this part of the coast. But Nature must certainly have changed her programme for 1884, for I have heard peals of thunder on several occasions since the Winter rains, one as late as June and—I am not keeping a meteorological record, and so may be mistaken—another in July.

Happening to be seated beside a window overlooking the Los Angeles Valley, picturesque with its groves of eucalypti and orange trees in the distance, I turned my eyes toward the sea after the tones rolled through the heavens. Sure enough!

there were unmistakable signs of a shower, and soon down came the welcome rain, delighting every body. Even the little birds were gleeful. Shortly then, uprose the sweet odors from the ground, the flowers, and trees. The dust nicely laid, the dark cloud swept off northward, hovering awhile over the summits of the San Fernando Mountains, and flashing out its crooked ribbons of fire.

"When he uttereth his voice there is a multitude of waters in the heavens." "He maketh lightnings with rain and bringeth forth the wind out of his treasures."

## XXV.

## A MINISTER TO THE LOWLIEST.

THE present Summer has witnessed a notable revival of interest in the early Spanish missions of Alta California. The feeling has been confined chiefly within the State, and particularly to the Catholic portion of the citizens, though some concern has been evinced beyond the border lines. The cause of this revival was the recurrence, on August 28th, of the one hundredth anniversary of their founder, the Rev. Junipero Serra, D. D.

For many weeks prior to that date the correspondents of the Pacific Coast newspapers were busy searching the archives and records of that early period; visiting the seats of the various missions; writing eloquent descriptions of their former wealth and present decay, and catechising the oldest living Spaniards, as well as the earliest pioneer Americans, for the purpose of bringing to light all the history of these stations and of their distinguished superintendent.

How much of permanent, practical good resulted

from the labors of this man among the wild Indian tribes whom he and his assistants found peopling this coast, and whom they subjugated in the name of the gospel and of the king of Spain, only a careful and impartial consideration of his methods, and of their immediate and later fruits, can determine. Certain it is, that viewed from this distance of time, and in the light of the fact that the tribes began to waste away almost from the hour the effort was inaugurated, those fifty or sixty years of Catholic attempt at uplifting and Christianizing the untutored race, form not a very satisfactory chapter in the history of civilization.

Nevertheless, the entire history of the period attests the fact that the Padre Junipero Serra himself ardently desired to be a true missionary of the cross and messenger of blessing to the rude red man. And if his work failed at all of the ends he sought, it should be attributed most to the methods and the paralyzing genius of the ecclesiastical power to which he was responsible. The eminent man lacked neither love for the Indian nor devotion to his work. This, all Californians concede, regardless of sect or creed. And unquestionably it was in reference to him, as a man who desired the good of the lowest of his race, and not as a priest of the

Catholic Church, that the citizens of the State, rather generally, were interested in the step to honor his memory. His name is inseparable from the early history of California, and in his personal record is the attraction of a spirit of great self-denial. For these reasons I take notice of this passing movement.

Junipero Serra was a native of the Island of Majorca, Spain, having been born November 24, 1713. He was small in stature, of feeble constitution, and "possessed a great love for books." Religiously inclined, he at the early age of seventeen applied to the order of Franciscans for membership. A year later he was admitted to full companionship in the fraternity, and addressed himself to the study of theology and philosophy, soon excelling as a teacher of these subjects. Immediately, also, he became celebrated as a pulpit orator, but, indifferent to the applause of city communities, he craved the privilege of preaching the gospel to the peasantry, especially desiring to minister to any who had never heard its conditions.

With this object in view he sailed for the New World, from Cadiz, August 28, 1749, and entered Mexico on New-Year's Day, 1750. Beginning missionary labors at once, and with great ardor, his name quickly became known in the Catholic Church of Mexico. After seventeen years of service in that part of the country, he was appointed president of the fifteen missions then existing in the Peninsula of California, and which had been founded by the Order of Jesuits, whom the government had just expelled. Here Serra found a field as needy, a people as abject, as he could wish for his training hand. It proved a territory far more difficult to cultivate than any the scholarly prelate had known, and in the course of time it was turned over to the Dominicans. Then, himself and sixteen subordinates set out on a missionary tour among the heathen tribes of Alta California.

Reaching the point on the coast where to-day stands the city of San Diego, seventeen miles north of the present frontier of Mexico, he there established, July 16, 1769, the first of the series of twenty-one missions embraced in what is now the State of California. The last of the series, that of San Francisco de Solano, was erected August 25, 1823. Ten years later this mission invoiced its possessions as follows: "Indian converts, fifteen hundred; cattle and horses, thirty-five hundred; goats and hogs, four thousand; fruits and grain, three thousand bushels. Nineteen years afterward, or in 1842, there were, it is said, but seventy Indians amenable to this mission.

From San Diego, whose mission church still stands, unroofed, with its walls crumbling to ruin, Father Serra moved northward to the lovely bay of Monterey. Here, June 3, 1770, he planted his second station, at the head of that sheet of water. Twelve months later the mission was transferred to the beautiful Carmelo Valley, some five miles down the coast from Monterey. Here, in time, rose a church edifice, a house for the priests, and barracks for the mission's handful of military protectors. These were all built of wood, and with the exception of the church, were covered with tules. The latter was roofed simply with earth.

From Carmelo it is claimed that Serra explored the coast as far northward as the fifty-fifth parallel, taking possession, "in the name of the Church and the King of Spain," of all the territory comprised in California, Oregon, and Washington. Returning to the mission on the Little Carmelo River, he there filled up the remainder of his days with self-denying labors among the surrounding Indian tribes; and there, greatly lamented by the simple-minded natives to whom he had faithfully ministered, he breathed his last, just one hundred years ago.

By his special request, his remains were interred "in the sanctuary of the church, on the gospel side of the altar." In the progress of years this building fell into decay, and was replaced by a structure of stone, erected on the same site, and covering the cherished remains of Junipero Serra. In turn this edifice also lapsed into ruin; and it is the question of its restoration which has this Summer drawn all Catholic eyes toward the little city of Monterey.

Recalling that the centennial of the great missionary's death was imminent, the pastor of the Catholic Church, at Monterey, "was moved early in the season to ask all Californians, irrespective of creed or color, to show respect to the man's memory, by handsomely restoring the ruin which had so long served as a monument over his grave." The newspapers took up his appeal; talked eloquently of the self-denying spirit of Padre Junipero Serra; of his manifold services to California and to its aboriginal tribes; of the fact that most of the missions he planted are well on the way to decay, and urged that the church at Carmelo should, out of gratitude, be preserved. The many Spaniards, Mexicans, and other Catholics of the coast were much aroused by these pleas, and contributed liberally to the object. Other citizens of the State also aided the cause generously.

Sufficient enthusiasm having been awakened to insure success, the work of renovation began, and in good time was completed. On the 28th of August, 1884, the old-new monument church was blessed with the customary Catholic ceremonial, many dignitaries of the Church being present, as were some State officials, and a large concourse of other persons. The ceremonies were of both a civic and religious character.

The renewal of the building was effected at a cost of sixteen thousand dollars, and now presents a curious mingling of ancient and modern architecture and decoration. The structure really serves the double purpose of a house of worship and a mausoleum. Upon the hearts of the Catholics the spot has a great hold. Through his whole life, I believe, Junipero Serra was a subject of great personal suffering, rendering his work all the more arduous. Certain it is that most of his days in California were passed in physical agony, which was partly the result of a frail constitution, and partly the fruit of exposure in founding the missions.

Of the twenty-one missions planted in Upper California, nine are said to have been established by Serra in person. These were, besides the two already named, that of San Juan Capistrano, the first station north of San Diego. The church is described as a splendid ruin. It was demolished by an earthquake one morning while mass was being celebrated, and the building was thronged with people. Thirty persons lost their lives, and many were injured. Services have always been held in one of its little chapels. "A priest resides there, and ekes out a scanty living by renting some of the crumbling rooms." That of San Gabriel, lying twelve miles east of Los Angeles, in one of the garden spots of Southern California; that of San Buena Ventura, near the sea-board, twenty-seven miles south of Santa Barbara; that of Santa Barbara itself, if I remember correctly, one of the richest of the series; that of San Antonio, located on the bank of a fine stream some miles from Soledad; that of San Luis Obispo, in the heart of the town of that name, and that of Santa Clara, three miles from San Jose. This church is a large structure, and "is the best preserved of the list." It once possessed a vast domain of productive acres.

Establishing the mission of San Buena Ventura was Padre Serra's last work in extending the realm of the Catholic Church. Twenty-eight months later, at Carmelo, he entered upon his final sleep. The Ventura mission was founded March 31, 1782, with jurisdiction over fifteen hundred square miles of territory. Before the sequestration of the missions it had acquired large possessions in flocks and herds also.

"The dominant idea in that really imposing missionary movement," said a gentleman yesterday, who, though not a Catholic, has through a long life been closely associated with members of that body, and has observed its methods of extending its power, "was, that within the period of one generation at most, whole tribes of the rude, idol-worshiping Indians could, under the teachings of the Church, the influence of the priests, and the restraints of the Spanish soldiery, be transformed into permanently civilized and Christianized societies. It was believed they could then be left to pursue works of piety and arts of peace under a civil administrator. The fatal defect in this reasoning was, to speak mildly, forgetfulness of the physiological fact that blood, which has been deteriorating through centuries of time, can not be restored to prime quality in the short space of forty or fifty years.

"As might have been foreseen, the whole scheme was a failure. And no person who has ever written upon the swift decadence of these Indian missions has touched the real cause. This, unquestionably, was their sequestration by the Mexican government. The moment the supreme control which the missionary fathers exercised over the neophytes of their respective stations was superseded by the rule of secular administrators, that moment the majority of the Indians left the missions and returned to the haunts of their ancestors, or sought employment on the ranchos of citizens friendly to them. Every attempt made between 1830 and 1840 to convert the neophytes into free and property-holding citizens, as was the case at the missions of San Diego, San Luis Rey, San Juan Capistrano, and San Juan Baptiste, proved miserable failures. The Indians soon showed that they had not acquired the power to retain the property left in their hands, nor to obtain more. It was the purpose of the Mexican government to leave in the hands of the converts all the land and other property belonging to the missions, as an outfit at the beginning of their self-governing career. But in a brief time the immense wealth of the stations was irrevocably scattered."

## XXVI.

## ROSES—PAMPAS GRASS—THE DATURA ARBOREA.

ONE of the chief attractions of Southern California is its beautiful and ceaseless product of flowers. Some of those which bloom the year round have a special season of efflorescence—a time when they reach their maximum of abundance and beauty. If I might select a single flower of which this is true, I should name the rose. The month of May is pre-eminently the rose period of the year, although there is never a day without them, and never a dearth of them.

A walk at evening, during this month, through some of the streets of Los Angeles inevitably brings to mind an enchanting story about the Vale of Cashmere, which I read in my childhood, in the State of New York. It was the power of contrast which made the story produce its ineffaceable impression upon my mind. I read it in midwinter. The snow covered the high rail fence which lined the public road leading to the country school which I attended. I walked to school on the crest of those snow-drifts. I read it before a great fire made of hickory logs, which snapped and hissed merrily in the big fire-place. The heat from it burned my round face, and warped the leather covers of the book. But I was wandering in a land flooded with sunshine, full of bloom, and breathing air laden with perfume. I wondered if the story were true; if I should ever see a land so fair; should smell roses so fragrant. Happily for my faith in that book, I now see roses as beautiful, breathe air as highly scented as ever floated over the sweet Vale of Cashmere.

On my way to Presbyterian prayer-meeting on Wednesday evenings I pass a beautifully kept ground, in which bloom, probably, a dozen varieties of roses. Among them are the Safrano, the Solfaterre, the bright Sanguinea, and the delicious Marechal Neil, besides five or six pink varieties, whose exquisite odor no language can describe. Climbing higher than any of the others, is the elegant Lamarque, pouring into the atmosphere from hundreds of blossoms a delightful perfume.

If I am alone, the moment I approach that yard I begin to walk slowly, and to take in great draughts of the fragrant air. When opposite some of the bushes I stand still, inhale the odor, and try to think what the perfume of flowers is. I recall all the words which have any aroma in them, and neither singly nor together do they express what I want to know. So I walk on, wishing it were a mile to the church, and that elegant roses lined all the way.

Yesterday afternoon an errand took me through Lower Third Street to Main. On one side stands a fine residence in the midst of trees and flowers. At the right of the entrance were a half-dozen rose-trees, four or five feet in height. The flexible branches bent under their burden of bloom. The warm air was dense with the mingled odors of the flowers. Separating this yard from its neighbor was a high fence. Over the top of it for many feet, down both its sides, and up among the branches of a cypress and another tree standing near, climbed a luxuriant Lamarque and a magnificent Cloth of Gold, both a mass of flowers, large and very double. It was a sight to make one stop and look.

In the adjoining yard was a cottage finished, with a veranda across the front. Up the pillars of the veranda, and over its roof the whole length, ran another Lamarque and a rich Marechal Neil. The result was a dense surface, from three to four feet wide by forty feet long, probably, of pure white and soft yellow flowers, the whole forming the most beautiful display of living roses I had ever seen. In the yard stood a Safrano rose-tree, five or more feet in height, and canopied with blossoms of matchless scent. Imagine those yards, that fence, that veranda! What a place for intoxicating the senses! What a pity that the Chinese—Americans, too—do not smoke rose-leaves!

It is quite customary on the Coast to compel rose-bushes to grow in the form of small trees. The effect is very pretty. At the top of a slender trunk shoot out a multitude of short branches, forming a canopy about the size of a sun-umbrella. Here the vitality centers, and, per consequence, the sprays are lavish in bloom. At the same time, the strength of the tree is well husbanded, for the moment a rose begins to fade it is removed, if the gardener does his duty.

Not far from where I write, is a rose tree, with trunk as large around as my arm. The first branches are some six feet above the ground, and are trimmed to present a flat surface to the sky. The effect is an even plane of delicate salmon-colored roses—a novelty even in Southern California.

A very charming class of roses to be seen here are the Banksias. There are three varieties, white, pink, and yellow, all bountiful bloomers and exceedingly fragrant. The blossoms are about the size of a large daisy, and usually are very double. They grow with astonishing rapidity. When riding into the country with a friend not long ago, she suddenly exclaimed, "Just look!"

Her object was to call my attention to a white banksia, which had climbed into the feathery top of a tall cypress, and then thrust its slender sprays all through the green boughs, so that they fell toward the ground on the side next the street, like a veil of snow. That, too, was a very striking sight.

Among the flowers which diffuse a fine perfume at night, as well as during the day, are the carnations, the orange blossoms, and the large, white, funnel-shaped blossoms of the Datura Arborea, a native of Peru and Columbia. The flowers consist of two corollas, one dropped within the other, as we would place a small funnel within a larger one. Both are ruffled slightly at the mouth, and remind one of the calla lily, but are far more delicate in texture. They hang pendulous from the branches of the trees, and will average nine inches in length. A number of the blossoms given me recently, measured twelve inches. I pass a Datura daily on my way to the post-office. From the lower branches, which strike out nearly at right angles from the trunk, depend a myriad of white, waxy-looking funnels. The fragrance from them never fails to send my imagination off on a trip to the Orient.

The carnations have a remarkably aromatic perfume which I have failed to notice in the pinks of the East. Nine handsome varieties flower beneath my windows, which are opened all night to let the breath of the beauties come in. What a sense of luxury they impart, perfuming one's very sleep!

Pampas plumes, the regal blossoms of the Gynerium Argenteum, made their appearance in the East but a few years ago. They were not then the article of commerce they now are. Usually they were seen only in homes where some member of the family had wandered away to this coast, and coming upon the elegant plant, had sent home one or two of the graceful flowers to adorn the best room. I well remember the first time I saw them. Three of the stately plumes drooped from a large vase in a friends' parlor. They were broad and heavy, with a rich cream color next the long stem, and a silver hue at the edges. They had a sort of royal look, as has a long ostrich plume.

The silver gynerium is a native of the pampas of Southern Brazil and lower plains of South America, where its appearance is very showy. As now cultivated in Southern California, it rivals the plant on its original prairies. Perhaps I can sketch the product for the reader. Imagine immense tufts of long, narrow, tough, finely saw-edged, green leaves, all sharply reflexed at the middle, and rising from the center of the tufts, fifty or one hundred splendid plumes or blossoms, averaging from two to three feet in length, and swaying from the top of slender stems twelve or fourteen feet in height. This paints you pampas grass as it may be seen here early in September, the time for harvesting the flowers, if I mistake not.

Heretofore Santa Barbara, ninety miles further north, has had the pre-eminence in the cultivation of this splendid plant. The climate being almost tropical, like that of Los Angeles, many foreign products, native to such latitudes, flourish there finely. This year, however, the florists of this city have rivaled it in the production of the gynerium. The blossoms of the Los Angeles seedling variety are the finest known on the coast. They are of a rich cream tint at the center, very feathery throughout, and measure from twenty-four to thirty-six inches in length. It is the unusual breadth of the flowers which distinguishes this variety.

### OTHER GYNERIUMS.

It is said that the great conservatories of Belgium grow not only the gynerium of this coast, but also some other varieties, the leaves of which are very handsome, being striped with white or yellow. It is doubtful, though, if these grasses belong to the same family as the Brazilian pampas. Very probably they belong to the Eulalia group, grasses which, in this country, are very effective in lawn ornamentation. In one variety bars of white cross the leaves, adding immensely to the beauty of the plant.

A fairly ornamental plant, possessing marked pampas characteristics, is produced now by eastern florists. It is a member of the Erianthus family, and like the true gynerium, may be propagated from the seed, or by dividing the root. The flower stems shoot up to a height of eight or ten feet, and the blossom makes a great effort to equal the plumes of the latter.

The South American pampas craves water. The result of liberal hydropathic treatment in its culture may be seen at a florist's on Los Angeles Street. One side the premises are bounded by a zanga.

through which flows a stream of muddy water from the irrigating reservoir. One bank of the stream is bordered with gigantic clumps of this plant. A forest of stems, topped out with regal plumes, rises from the midst of each. So interwoven are the saw-edged leaves that to pass between the tufts is an impossibility.

## XXVII.

## WOMEN AS CULTIVATORS OF THE SOIL.

ONE day in June last the writer was one of a dozen passengers in the "morning stage" from Los Angeles to Pasadena. The vehicle was not one of those oval-shaped, springy, swaying coaches which, as I fancied in my childhood, insure the very perfection of carriage riding, and which the traveler of the present day may test, should he ever cross the rugged Siskiyou Mountains in one of the coaches of the Oregon and California stage-line, but was a long, four-seated conveyance, with high, square top and open sides. From it we could obtain a fine view of the picturesque country for miles around.

The passengers were all in their seats only one-half hour after the time, and presently the four-in-hand dashed off from the *cigar-store* in Temple Block, claiming to be the head-quarters of the stage company. The little seven-by-nine room is by no means a pleasant waiting point for ladies, and I being usually ahead of time when setting out on such a jaunt, had the pleasure of seeing no end of money set fire to, in little slender rolls of tobacco, during the hour I watched for the stage.

The morning was cloudy. The atmosphere was laden with chilling moisture, which the breeze drove sharply into our faces. Anywhere in the East, under such circumstances, an all-day rain might confidently have been predicted; but in Southern California it "never rains when it does," so we were not disappointed to see the mist drift away long before noon. Then down came the genial sunlight, making the earth and ourselves rejoice.

Our road twice crossed the Arroyo Secco, a chatty stream flowing from the Sierra Madre. All around, the country was covered with wrinkles, like an aged face furrowed by years of care. Now we sped across a pretty valley, decked with venerable live-oaks, ever green, and singularly effective in the landscape, but some of them painfully distorted in shape. Now we were borne up a long hill, from whose top we had a view of scenes quite worthy the brush which put the Yo-Semite on canvas.

Upon the seat beside me sat an intelligent lady from some town in Iowa. She had been on a visit to Elsinore, a new colony springing up, with fair prospects, not far from Riverside. Her husband, as I soon learned, was one of its projectors, and, as was entirely proper, she appeared to be much interested in the sale of Elsinore lots. She quietly advised a young man, forming the third party on our seat, and evidently just catching the real-estate fever, to "see Elsinore before investing elsewhere in Southern California." That was kind of her. The new town occupies a location as charming as is its name, on the border of Elsinore Lake, where it would be delightful to dwell. The place has advantages all its own, and might exactly meet the wants and means of this stranger. If so, two men had been helped.

It is very noticeable how quickly bright-minded women from other parts of the country become interested, and then engaged, in real-estate transactions on this coast. It is worthy of remark, too, what ability they display in the business, and what success they achieve. Some one has said that as large a proportion of women as men, increase their fortunes by this sort of trade. They are quick to discern the favorable or unfavorable points in a piece of property, and seem to know when they have received a good offer from a purchaser.

A friend recently informed me that of a certain

large tract of land near the city, which was put on the market lately in small lots, nearly one-half the buyers were women; and also, that it is not a rare thing for numbers of feminine speculators to attend the auction sales of land frequently taking place, and to bid quietly but intelligently for the property.

Of the sixty-five or more women employed as teachers in the public schools of Los Angeles, there is scarcely one who is not the owner of land somewhere in the State. Numbers of women on the coast—in California, in Oregon—personally superintend considerable farms, the titles to which are in their own name. They themselves make the sales of the crops. In some instances they have brought their land up to a high figure by putting it under fine cultivation. Of the five women who happen to be at this moment in the house where I write, all possess land in or near the city.

Much has been said about an educated and sensible young woman who, with her invalid father, resides in one of the colonies not very distant from Los Angeles. She is the owner of a raisin vineyard of ten or more acres, every vine in which was planted by her own hands. The vineyard is now in full bearing. Every year she superintends the picking, curing, and packing of her crop, and makes her own terms with the dealers. I think she is the possessor also of ten acres of orange trees, in thrifty condition. The story goes that when the little cottage in which they live was in process of erection, the roof being unfinished, a severe storm threatened. This made it necessary for the father—his own carpenter, I presume—to have aid in the shingling. None being obtainable in the small town, the indomitable girl climbed to the roof, and laid shingles until the work was complete, acquitting herself as creditably at carpentry as she does at raisin-making.

I am now obliged to add that, no sooner had this brave, energetic girl acquired her pretty home, and become well advanced toward competency, than there chanced that way a Methodist minister, who, admiring her noble qualities, invited her to become his wife. And she, pleased with the idea, accepted the invitation, and is about to be married.

In the same village live two sisters, young women from Wisconsin, who, with a widowed mother, came to the place but a few years ago. With their slender means they purchased a few acres of land near, and soon had growing upon it a raisin vineyard and an orange grove, much of the labor of planting them being performed with their own hands. While their vines and trees were growing, one of them, a girl rarely endowed, applied for the position of postmaster in the community, and received the appointment, "her application being indorsed by nearly every voter in the town."

About this time the Southern Pacific Railway, learning that she was an accomplished telegrapher, gave her important employment in that occupation, her sister becoming her efficient deputy in the post-office. These young women are the daughters of a Congregational clergyman who died some years ago, and are, of course, cultured, Christian girls. Their womanly ways, promptness, and conscientious discharge of duty, as daughters, in the Church, in society, in business, have won them the good will and respect of all parties. As a result of economy and judicious investments in real estate, their combined fortune now, at the close of about five years, amounts to some sixteen thousand dollars.

We are now well on the way to Pasadena. Suddenly the four-in-hand wheel into a flower-bordered drive-way on our right. Then comes to view a trim little cottage crowning one of the "wrinkles." Now out of the front door-way bound two or three young children, shouting "Mamma!" After them comes a babe in somebody's arms. The place was the home, these were the children, of the lady from Elsinore. Ourselves happy over the welcome she received, we bade her adieu, turned back to the main road, and began climbing Hermosa Vista Hill, one of the sightliest eminences in all this picturesque region, and, as has been said in a previous chapter, the seat of a college for young men.

The summit gained, a short time brought us into Orange Grove Avenue, the finest street in Pasadena. Throughout its entire length vineyards, orange groves, inviting grounds, and comfortable abodes grace both sides. Speeding on a couple of miles, we at last turned into the broad, arched gateway at Carmelita, the beautiful home of Dr. Ezra S. Carr and his family. Here the stage left the writer for a twenty-four hours' sojourn. As we wound through the drive-way to the house, we noticed among the great variety of choice trees in the grounds, cedars from Lebanon, India, Norway, Oregon, and the Norfolk Islands; also, the maple, butternut, mulberry, palm, bamboo, several species of eucalypti—natives of Australia—and the sturdy sequoia, of Calaveras stock, with other home and foreign trees.

Carmelita is intended to suggest not only the name of its proprietor, but also Mount Carmel, in

Syria. Naturally it calls up the days of Elijah, and the scenes of the august miracle which took place on that summit, with its attendant human slaughter. The cottage, framed in with flowers and vines, occupies the crown of a long descent toward the east. In the foreground, on that side, stands an apricot orchard in splendid condition. Beyond that, a part of the lovely village comes into the picture. Farther away, stretches the rich San Gabriel Valley. On the left, three miles distant, rise the stately Sierra Madre Mountains. Thus are brought into the beautiful panorama the extremes of scenery. Walking about the perfect grounds to-day, noting the scope of the improvements on every hand, it is difficult to persuade one's self that seven years have sufficed to produce fruit and forest trees of such magnitude; and still more difficult to believe the whole is the result of one little woman's effort.

Seven years ago—this account was penned in 1884—Doctor Carr and his family were living in the city of Sacramento, himself being the State Superintendent of Public Instruction. With health impaired by forty years of arduous labor in educational fields, he was admonished that a retreat where rest could be assured, would soon become a necessity. This led to the purchase of the forty acres now constituting Carmelita. They were then a mere barren waste. Not a furrow had ever been turned upon them. Soon after they were acquired Mrs. Carr left her home in Sacramento, came to Pasadena, set men to breaking up the soil on this place, built a temporary habitation for her family, laid out these now beautiful grounds, and from that time, with great energy, carried forward her improvements. At that time Mrs. Carr was the Assistant State Superintendent of the Public Schools of California. For years she had been associated with her husband in educational work.

On many occasions during this period had women of culture and ability sought her advice, with reference to earning a livelihood for themselves. In reply she had often urged the obtaining a support from the soil, in some one of the many pleasant departments of horticulture possible in California. Most, if not all of them, had lacked the courage to make the attempt. In the development of her forty acres, therefore, she determined to furnish them a practical illustration of the views she had advocated. And, to-day, Carmelita, with its many different lines of production, is her noble, self-denying answer to a multitude of women desirous of learning how they may support themselves, and provide something for the future.

Mrs. Carr has endeavored to exemplify what a woman may accomplish on a few acres of land in one, two, three, and four years, with much or with little capital. The particulars of her effort are as interesting as useful, but must be excluded from this volume. Suffice it to say that Carmelita is, in many of its departments, a splendid object-lesson for women having families of children to support. It is a favorite project in the mind of Mrs. Carr to some day convert Carmelita into a State school of horticulture for women. May she live to do it!

Of Pasadena itself all the world has heard; how attractive it is; how delightfully situated, at the head of the fair San Gabriel Valley; and how, in the space of a few swift years, it sprang from a desert state into square miles of vineyards and orchards of all kinds. It is the gem of Southern California towns, and will long remain such. Tourists can find no lovelier place to winter in. But the man of limited means, seeking a home there for his family, would be shut out by the high price of land.

## XXVIII.

## SAN PEDRO.

SAN PEDRO is a name one hears daily in Southern California. Every traveler, bound up or down the coast by sea, and desiring to reach Los Angeles, must enter the place *via* San Pedro. Or, being already in the thriving metropolis, and wishing to journey by water to any point along the shore, it is San Pedro which opens the door and lets him out. To a great extent Australian coalfields furnish the citizens of Los Angeles their fuel. But it can glow on their hearths only after a handsome fee for lighterage has been paid this town.

San Pedro is the sea-port of Los Angeles County, and is therefore a place of some importance, though but a mere hamlet in size. I had spent thirteen months in this part of the State, and had not seen the locality. So one morning last week, a very dear friend accompanying me, I determined to make the southward run to the sea. Accordingly, at half-past nine o'clock we were at the Commercial Street depot, in Los Angeles, waiting for the train. Every morning about that hour four trains halt there, bound to as many different parts of the country. The small waiting-room was crowded with travelers, collected from every quarter of the city. Outside, under the extended roof of the building, were congregated nearly as many more, Americans, Mexicans, Germans, Italians, Chinese, and negroes, the same incongruous assembly one sees on all such occasions in any of these coast towns.

It was interesting to watch them. They were doing almost as many different things as there were persons—reading, talking, calculating with a pencil, entering memoranda in note-books, buying tickets, changing money, moving baggage, studying the costumes of the women. One man, with fiery red hair, a hard, freckled face, and an expression of the eye which made one feel sick and turn away, seated himself directly opposite us, and immediately opened a small bag filled with Muscat grapes, which he began to devour greedily. Seeds, pulp, and tough skin were relished alike. No wonder the man's face wore both a pale and painful look. That was one of nature's punishments for his lack of obedience to her laws. He deserved it.

Just as our train appeared in sight, far down Alameda Street, a fruit-vender drove up in front of the station, with a load of pomegranates, the first I had seen in California. The fruit was about the shape and size of the common quince, of a golden, yellow color on one side, and rose-tinted on the other. Inside the pomegranate is filled with bright, red seeds, nearly flat, and as large as those of a small watermelon. Filled in between them is the pleasant, sweetish, cooling pulp, so grateful to the taste in warm Asiatic climates. The pomegranate is cultivated with success in this section of the State, and in increasing quantities. To what use it is put, except the making of refreshing drinks, and eating out of hand, I have not learned. I admired the sample handed me by my friend for its beauty, and regarded it with interest, on account of its Bible associations; but upon trying to eat it, concluded that an orange, an apricot, or a banana were ever so much more agreeable to my taste.

"Let us take seats in the last car," said Mrs. H—, as we stepped aboard the train, "for from the rear door we can obtain a view of the whole country, and that is what you want."

To that part of the train, therefore, we betook ourselves, and soon were speeding through the suburbs of the city, with acres of vineyards, orange groves, walnut and apricot orchards, bounding the track on either side. The charm of these fruit fields continued for five or six miles out. Then the scene changed, and we flitted past a succession of extensive ranchos. Around the residences upon them rose small forests of eucalypti, planted as much for effect in the landscape as for protection against the sun and wind. The eucalyptus is *the* tree of Southern California for elegance and style, unless the dracœna or fan-palm are its rivals in these respects. As unlike as possible in height, form, and foliage, they all are extremely, though differently, effective in expansive grounds. Each studied as it deserves, awakens lofty thoughts. The springs of poetry are in all of them. Though seen every day, they are the same impressive objects. One never tires of them. In that happy day when "all the trees of the field shall clap their hands," may the eucalyptus, dracœna, and fan-palm help make the music!

Again the panorama changes, and we have a vision of broad, bare, brown hills, slopes, and levels, off westward; but toward the south a picture of smooth water, blue as the cloudless sky over our heads. It is San Pedro Bay. Now we rumble into Wilmington, situated at the head of tide-water on Wilmington Bay, or "the inner harbor," as it is often called, and five miles from the anchorage of the great ocean ships and steamers. It is approaching eleven o'clock in the morning, and the tide is now in, making the little place look attractive with its foreground of shimmering sea. But wait until we return this afternoon, then we shall find it high and dry on the edge of a long stretch of wet marsh and mud. In 1882.an act of Congress established the "customs district of Wilmington," making the place the port of entry for Southern California, and Hueneme, Santa Barbara, and San Buena Ventura its ports of delivery. The young town has a fair prospect of growth.

But it is the grand old ocean itself we desire to see, and so we continue our ride three miles and a half over a row of piles standing deep in water to San Pedro, close to the sea, but sheltered from the furious north-west winds by a high bluff on the right, and commanding a magnificent view of the outer bay, the roadstead, and that "classic mound" at the mouth of the harbor, called Dead Man's Island.

The bay of San Pedro sets up into the mainland from the Pacific in a north-easterly direction, and from east to west is three and one-half miles wide.

Back from its shores some distance lie the flourishing towns of Orange, Tustin, Santa Ana, and Westminster. While hugging the water's edge, almost due east of San Pedro, can be discerned "Long Beach," a new Summer resort in high favor among lovers of sea-side pleasures throughout all this region. And away to the southward thirty-five miles, out of sight, stand the interesting ruins of the old mission of San Juan Capistrano.

Our train drawing up alongside the dock of the Pacific Coast Steamship Company, we tarried a few moments to see our fellow passengers, most of whom were bound up the coast, embark on board the transport which was to convey them off to the great steamer *Santa Rosa*, anchored in the roadstead, and pouring from her tall, black pipes columns of dense smoke into the pure salt-scented air. Then turning away we walked up the beach a half-mile or less, to Timms' Point, where stand the pleasant home of Captain Timms, once the owner of six thousand acres adjoining the point, a cottage occupied by a Presbyterian minister and his family, from Pasadena, and those of one or two other parties who had come to the spot for a new lease of life. Seated on the porch of the captain's cottage, and looking southward we had an extended view of the sea and outer bay. In the harbor, besides the *Santa Rosa*, lay a number of large merchant ships—five of them English—which had come in freighted with coal from Australia, and having discharged their cargoes, were loading with wheat grown in the Cahuenga, Los Angeles, and San Gabriel Valleys. Both these commodities were conveyed, the one from, the other to, the ships by transports at great expense. Upon every ton of coal from Australia, unladed at the port, the government receives a duty of seventy-five cents.

From Dead Man's Island, at the very mouth of the harbor and just in front of the cottage, there stretches to Rattlesnake Island, a low, sandy reach of land in the northern part of the outer bay, a costly breakwater, one mile and a quarter in length, on which the government has expended three-fourths of a million of dollars, in order to provide a channel of sufficient depth to float up to the docks at San Pedro the largest ocean vessels. As yet the work proves but a partial success, and there are persons who openly assert that the object can never be attained with the breakwater in its present position. Some distance from Timms' Point, on the west, a head of land makes out into the ocean, from which, it is said, if the defense had been constructed to Dead Man's Island, a harbor would have been secured capacious and deep enough to have admitted all the shipping likely to visit the port at any one time. As it is, the north-west wind, which almost talks around these points, drives the sand into the channel, necessitating constant dredging to preserve a passage that will admit lumber vessels and steamers of ordinary size. The last Congress appropriated $75,000 to continue the improvement of the harbor.

Captain Timms proved to be an old sailor, who possessed a bountiful experience of ocean life and hardships, besides a fund of knowledge of foreign countries. By birth he is a Prussian. In 1844 he entered the American merchant-marine service, while a mere youth, remaining four years. Then he accompanied the benevolent-hearted master of some ship, to his home in Portland, Maine, and under his direction studied navigation, together with the rudimentary branches of an English education. In 1849, leaving New York as the mate of a vessel, he came to the Pacific Coast, made an attempt at mining, met with no success, and disliking the business, went to San Francisco, and engaged with certain shipping firms of that city to act as their agent in San Pedro. Hither he came in 1852, bidding sailor life a lasting farewell, and establishing himself as a commission merchant, or general business man of the region. Here, in sight of the sea, with the woman who came, a young girl, from the far-off home land, to marry him, he has lived thirty-four years. The captain's house is built partly upon a government transport, which, during the war with Mexico in 1846, steamed into this bay freighted with troops bound for Los Angeles to reenforce General Kearney, then in command there. After the soldiers disembarked the vessel parted her chains in a storm and went ashore under the bluff on our right. Sometime subsequently she was floated into the harbor for repairs, but was condemned instead. About this date Captain Timms was meeting with some opposition from the Mexicans of the vicinity, who did not relish his movements for permanent settlement among them. So, wishing to avoid a collision, he erected his dwelling over the abandoned transport, holding that it was American territory.

The argument was a success, and they ceased to molest him. All these years the wind and the waves have been making land in front of his home, and to-day the old transport lies firmly imbedded in sand and pebbles several rods back from its native element.

"For twenty-five years after we came here," said the urbane captain, "we brought all the water we used for cooking and drinking a distance of three miles. Now we get it from the railway reservoir, a half-mile away."

Dead Man's Island, just before us, and containing less than an acre of ground, received its name, it is said, from the circumstance that when on the march towards Los Angeles, the troops above mentioned had an engagement with the Mexican force and suffered a loss of fifteen men. The bodies of the slain were returned to San Pedro and interred near this point. At this the natives were much incensed, and declared that if the bodies were not removed they should be thrown over the high bluff into the sea. Thereupon the dead were exhumed and re-buried on this little hillock rising out of the water.

It was in the bay of San Pedro, and on board the little brig *Pilgrim*, from Boston, while she lay anchored off shore, near where, to-day, float these seven large merchantmen, that took place that cruel and disgraceful flogging scene which Mr. Richard Henry Dana so thrillingly describes in his "Two Years Before the Mast." Here the commander of the brig, Captain Thompson, with barely the shadow of a reason for his cruel deed, and with his own hands, punished two of his crew until their bodies were lacerated and dripping with blood; and, as if that were torture insufficient, he immediately upon releasing them, ordered his boat lowered and commanded the wounded men to bear a hand in rowing him to shore, three miles and a half distant! That barbarity occurred fifty-one years ago, but the memory of it lingers about this harbor still, and will be vividly called up by every reader of Mr. Dana's most interesting book who chances to visit San Pedro.

San Pedro lies twenty-one miles south of Los Angeles, occupies a sightly situation, is a pleasant sea-side resort, has a few hundred inhabitants, three churches, two public school-houses, and is the southern terminus of the Southern Pacific Railway.

## XXIX.

## IN THE SANTIAGO CAÑON.

SOME one has said that "prisons are not the abodes of wicked men only." Equally true is it that mountain fastnesses are not the retreats of criminals solely. Men and women have languished long in cells and dungeons for no other reason than because they opposed wrong and approved of right. So have men and women spent their lives in secluded gorges, on lonely mountain sides, not because they had infringed the laws, or were hiding from justice, but for reasons as right as are the motives which lead other people to settle on plains or in valleys. There are persons who crave a life among Nature's wild scenes. The nearer her rough, honest heart they can get the happier they are. Never is her visage harsh or repellent to them. Marred or fair, in repose or swept by storms, it is beautiful.

Nor does it follow that these lovers of Nature are indifferent to the affairs of the great family of man to which they belong. They are lovers of their race as well. Molinos once said: "Whoever wounds the Church of God wounds me." So whatever concerns the human race, concerns these great-hearted dwellers among the everlasting hills, and some of them manage to send down, or carry down, from their lofty nooks a vast deal of help for the needy world. Though themselves cabined in pure air, they do not forget the multitudes tented amid the earth's moral miasms below. Never are they the people to say: "What matters it to us whether men are blessed or wretched?"

It is in such a mountain home, among such helpful people, that I pen these lines this morning. Or rather it is in the door-yard, seated in the shade of a spreading live-oak tree, through whose branches falls the yellow sunlight, in flickering patches, on the smooth, hard ground. Close by stands the tiny cottage, with its green blinds, its numerous porches and outer doors. Near the dwelling, supported by nine slender posts, is a square roofing of live-oak branches laid thickly together. The posts are twined with water ivy and other climbing vines. The space sheltered by this canopy is the dining-room. In the center stands a large table, at which we have just taken a delicious breakfast of coffee, hot rolls, fresh cheese, and thick white honey from the apiary, in sight across the creek which flows down the cañon. For this dining-room Nature wove the carpet. Disdaining cotton or wool, she made it of the earth, and took pleasure in the thought that the feet of men and women can never wear the staunch fabric thread-bare. Feet may come and feet may go, but that carpet will wear forever.

Adjoining the dining-room is the kitchen, without vestige of walls. In other words, the cooking-stove is overarched by a glossy live-oak, the heavens overarching that. The short pipe is kept in place by an ingenious contrivance, as follows: Two slender poles have an end of each nailed to separate trees near, in such manner as to cross and fasten nicely just in front of the pipe, while a cross-piece holds them in place back of the pipe. There is a twofold advantage in this arrangement. First, it is economical; second, when the stove goes into the house, as it will at the approach of cold weather, it will be but the work of a moment to send the poles flying; then the remainder of the work is *easy*.

Nor must it be inferred that kitchen pantries have been omitted in this plan for open-air house-keeping. Three or four cases of shelves conveniently placed, some with doors, some without, one secured to a strong tree, another set upon a couple of boxes, supply every want of that character.

The cottage stands on a mere green shelf in the cañon, sixteen miles from its mouth. Westward from it stretches a narrow plateau adorned with grand live-oaks, a number of them growing in families from one root. Fifteen or twenty feet back of the dwelling rises a steep, semi-circular wall of mountain, and immediately back of that a lofty cone towering to a height of 5,500 feet above the sea. Across the cañon, here about six hundred feet wide, a second summit sends its crest toward the sky. Beyond and north of that stretches up cone after cone in noble array, while farther up the gorge, which narrows every rod of the distance, height crowns height in sublime succession. All around is majesty and grandeur. This is no place for the wicked. A fugitive from the law would be miserable here. Only the good and the true can be in harmony with these massive works of the Almighty. Round and about these immutable peaks winds Santiago Creek; washing this plateau within a few rods of my feet, and sending over to me, from among its rocks and stones, a gleeful "Good morning." At this season of the year—October—it is a harmless stream; but let a characteristic Southern

California rain descend for a week, and it would foam, and tumble, and revel in the midst of ruin.

The proprietors of this delightful home, and of many acres of this splendid scenery, are Mr. and Mrs. J. E. Pleasants, both of genuine pioneer stock and well known among the old families of the coast. In fulfillment of a promise to visit them, made some weeks ago, I am now here, and am enjoying more than words can express the bracing mountain air, the songs of the birds, and the absence of all city sounds and voices. No wonder the Son of man craved the quietude of the mountains, and the rest of "sweet Galilee, where he so much loved to be." Rest, strength, and inspiration are in these heights, in this stream.

Sometime in 1883 there arrived on this part of the coast a young man by the name of Carpenter, from Kentucky. He engaged in business in Los Angeles, acquired quite a fortune, and became the possessor of an extensive tract of land in the vicinity of Los Nietos, which was for many years known as "Carpenter's Rancho." In the course of time he married a young lady by the name of Dominguez, a Spanish family then notable in Los Angeles and Santa Barbara counties. This couple were the parents of Mrs. Pleasants. Her early home was the Los Nietos rancho. Much pains was taken with the young lady's education, and she reached womanhood possessed of intelligence, broad views, and a kindly heart. She, of course, speaks the language of both her father and mother.

The parents of Mr. Pleasants, both Americans, emigrated to the northern portion of the State from the East before there existed the faintest token of California's present enterprise and greatness, and at a period when it required great heroism to make a stand for a home and subsistence in that part of the coast. Hostile Indians and savage beasts lurked on every hand. At the age of twelve young Pleasants was sent down to Los Angeles to attend school in the family of William Wolfskill, a personal friend of his father, and at that time the owner of leagues of this Santiago Mountain chain, and of the fair and fertile Valley of Santa Ana spreading out from their base. Mrs. Wolfskill was herself a Dominguez. Maria Refugio Carpenter was her relative, and a pupil in the Wolfskill school. Years went by. Young Pleasants became attached to Southern California and to Maria Carpenter, and concluded to remain indefinitely. To assist him in carrying out this resolution, Mr. Wolfskill proposed his coming down into this section of the country to look after the flocks and herds roaming over the vast Wolfskill estate.

The proposal was accepted, and soon the young man found himself leading an easy, fascinating kind of life; one strongly spiced with danger, indeed, but not more objectionable on that account. Mounted upon a fleet, intelligent horse, he rode up and down these wild cañons, to and fro over the lonely mountains, back and forth on the grassy plains, day after day. Thus sped several years. Greater grew the charm of the mountains, more repulsive the thought of spending life in some pent-up town or city. Finally Maria Carpenter concluded that it would be pleasant to change her name. So, seven years ago, the two, made one, pitched their tent on this little green shelf in the Santiago cañon; gave it the name of Pleasant Refuge; made it bright with books, pictures, and flowers, and made their lives useful, as well by dispensing here a delightful hospitality, as by heartily forwarding the interests of society in county and State.

The cottage is located about three miles from the head of the cañon. From Santa Ana, the nearest town, it is distant twenty-three miles, and from Los Angeles sixty. It is neither a hotel nor a boarding-house, but the quiet home of a private family.

And yet to the sunny nook come old and young, sick and well, tired and hungry, strangers and acquaintances, the simple and the gifted, all feeling assured of a hearty welcome. When urged, as he sometimes is, to convert his residence into a resort for the public, and take compensation for meals, lodging, and provender for the teams of guests, Mr. Pleasants always replies:

"I can't do that. I like to make people happy. Every body is welcome."

And Mrs. Pleasants, always in perfect accord with her husband on this point, says: "Our house is capable of enlarging itself to almost any size; and then it is quite worth while to live to help people on their way," or something to that effect.

But not always do guests come uninvited. Some are welcomed out of a great love for them in the hearts of Mr. and Mrs. Pleasants. This is true, for instance, whenever Madame Modjeska, Count Bozenta, her husband, and their son Rudolph, come into this gorge for a month's recreation, as they do whenever their engagements call them to this part of the world. It may not be well known that Madame Modjeska and her husband, desiring that their son should be reared under American institutions, and become a citizen of the United States, left Europe permanently as they supposed, came to Southern California, purchased property at or near Anaheim, and settled down to pass the remainder of their days in quiet. Three years went by. The competency they possessed at their coming had taken wings and disappeared. This misfortune induced the gifted woman to seek the stage again. It is comforting to know, when you are a wanderer in distant lands, that only just words will be spoken of you by the friends from whom duty forced you to turn away. Such friends had Modjeska in the Santiago Cañon, when she went out to rebuild the fortune wrecked in the Santa Ana Valley.

During the Industrial Exhibition at New Orleans Mr. Pleasants was commissioned by the Southern California Bee Association to act as the superintendent of the honey exhibit from this part of the State. He conveyed to the Crescent City a complete line of honey plants native to the region, together with a magnificent display of the product itself, and sample colonies of the three races of bees at work on the coast. Mr. Pleasants spent some months in New Orleans, calling the world's attention to the fact that nowhere does there grow a greater variety of rich bee food, and nowhere is there made a finer quality of honey, than in Southern California. The supply of food is almost, if not quite, perennial, the flowers of one set of plants coming forward as soon as others disappear. Notable among them are the blossoms of the four sages—the white, black, silver, and hybrid; also, the wild sumac, wild coffee-plant, golden rod, wild alfalfa, wild buckwheat, and many others. These were shown mostly in a living state in New Orleans, so that persons interested might see how they look. Not only the Santiago range, but most of the mountains of Southern California teem with honey plants. The San Fernando chain is especially prolific of such growths.

## XXX.

## A WONDERFUL FLOWER FESTIVAL.

THE devoting a chapter of this work to a Southern California floral display simply, may seem like an inconsiderate waste of time and space; but when I state that the exhibition was probably the most extraordinary affair of the kind that ever occurred, that fact will be received as a sufficient apology for inserting an acount of it. Should the reader, upon reaching the end of the chapter, regret that circumstances did not call him to Los Angeles last Spring, let me remind him that a similar magnificent *fete* will be given in that city for several years to come, and each will probably exceed in loveliness the one of which I am about to write. Thus opportunity will be afforded to retrieve one's loss in this respect.

Beautiful exhibitions of cut flowers and growing plants have been witnessed in California for a number of years past. Santa Barbara has rivaled the coast in the elegance and magnitude of her displays, until Los Angeles tried her hand at the lovely labor in April, 1886. Then Santa Barbara lost her pretty pre-eminence, and all the rest of America was eclipsed. The prestige then gained, quite unexpectedly to herself, Los Angeles proposes, albeit very courteously, to retain. The complete success achieved last April is evidence that this will not be difficult to do.

There exists in Los Angeles an organization whose object is, to aid poor women in the city who are compelled to toil for daily bread, and especially women who are strangers. Sincere and earnest in their purpose, the ladies who formed the organization two years ago set about ascertaining the extent of their field. To their surprise they found in the city a large number of women whose earnings were so meager as to preclude the possibility of their living comfortably. Not a few were young women in frail health, who had come to the coast from all parts of the country, in the hope of regaining strength, but lacked the means to remain long without some occupation. Unable to forget their pathetic discoveries, these women determined to establish a home where those whose cases appealed most strongly to their sympathies, should be furnished the comforts and pleasures they required, at very small cost.

So, taking the name of the Flower Festival Society, they resolved to give annually, for some time, a grand floral entertainment, devoting the proceeds to this purpose. An effort, which netted them a handsome sum was made in the Spring of 1885, and in the Autumn of that year followed an art loan exhibition, which also proved a great success financially, and at the same time a source of many-sided education to the public. How it was possible, even for women so determined, to pick up in a city no larger than Los Angeles, the extensive collection of rare, curious, and beautiful articles, many of which were of great interest on account of their age, history, or intrinsic value, was a mystery.

It was not dreamed, until the work of centralization began, what a wealth of rich relics, curios, souvenirs, and heir-looms were hidden away in the homes of this promiscuous people. All lands had a share in the display. Kings, and grandees, and warriors, and skillful old art-workers lived again in the garments and ornaments, etchings, engravings, paintings, carvings, and books of a past day. If the exhibit proclaimed any thing, it was, that away down in this south-western corner of our country dwells a community possessed of taste, culture, and a veneration for the wonderful handicraft and head-craft of the human race. Families brought out for an airing, articles skillfully devised by savants and savages, priests and prisoners, all showing that, spite of the defacings of sin, man retains something, mentally, of the image of God in which he was made.

This over, the Winter was given to preparations for the event of the Spring. The tabernacle erected by the churches of Los Angeles for the meetings of Dr. Munhall in the Autumn, and having a capacity for seating five thousand persons, was engaged for the occasion. The next step was to form the plan of the festival. And herein, as well as in its successful execution, was manifested the marked ability of the society. The ladies determined what features the exhibition should comprise, besides that of the flowers, and placed each department in charge of some woman of well-known responsibility and executive talent, leaving her to select her own assistants, and to conduct its affairs to the end, according to her own judgment. Then a gentleman who combined the qualifications of an architect and of a landscape gardener was engaged to construct the necessary booths, and dispose them in the building with a view to picturesque and landscape effects. Next, a list was made of the parties in the city, vicinity, and surrounding towns, who would without fail contribute flowers during the two weeks' display, and also of the kinds of flowers they would furnish. This known, the city and country were districted, and the days assigned for calling upon each party for its contributions. Also, committees were appointed to collect the flowers in each district on the days specified. The object of all these steps was to insure a sufficient supply of flowers to effect a complete renewal of the exhibit every day; and this most astonishing feat was actually accomplished.

Let the reader imagine the magnitude of the task of replacing thousands upon thousands of slightly withered blossoms, in a multitude of intricate and elaborate designs, every morning before ten ten o'clock. Furthermore, conceive of a country which could yield the lovely products in such profusion that the change could even be thought of. And think of the daring and energy of the women, who, without precedent, ventured to make the attempt.

The plan inside the tabernacle embraced thirty-four booths. Among them were those named for the towns of Tustin, Orange, Santa Ana, Pasadena, San Gabriel, Boyle Heights, San Buena Ventura, and others, all of which were daily supplied with fresh flowers and other attractions from these communities, thus preserving their loveliness to the end. The Tustin booth was conspicuous for its beauty, being kept filled with gems of the florist's art. One of its marvels was a collection of pansies of every known color, kept daily renewed. Another was a miniature house, with walls of sweet alyssum, roof of red geraniums, and cornice of heliotrope. The columns of its piazza were wreated with smilax. The house stood on a hill-side built of geraniums. Leading up to the front door was a pathway paved with fragrant banksia roses. Inside the lovely structure appeared floral designs made solidly of either heliotrope, banksia roses, waxy calla lillies, or starry marguerites, with not a wilted blossom among them during the entire exhibit. San Gabriel showed a representation of its old mission church, built of tuberoses, alyssum, geraniums, and other effective blooms. But the Ventura booth, with its source of supply at least ninety miles distant, carried off the palm for enterprise. Invoices of fresh flowers were dispatched from that town every afternoon at five o'clock, and in twenty-three hours were delivered at the tabernacle, fifty miles of the journey having been accomplished by teams and the remainder by rail.

At the booth devoted to oranges, trim cones, cubes, and pyramids of the royal fruit vanished daily with the sun. At one or more booths exquisite corsage and button-hole bouquets, with little fancy baskets of flowers, were retailed in great numbers, keeping constantly employed in their manufacture the deft fingers of a committee for the purpose. Besides these booths, a number were devoted exclusively to the sale and exhibition of loose cut-flowers and growing plants. Here the lovely creations were furnished the purchaser in any form to suit his fancy, at any price, of any variety. This required no small investment in twine, tin-foil, and other appliances for instantly constructing hand bouquets. A great demand was created for the yellow marigold for corsage decoration. Among roses, strong preference was shown for the beautiful zenwood, a flower having nearly the same characteristics as the safrano, except that its color is a shrimp pink.

How general, and how warm, was the interest taken in the *fête* itself, as well as in its object, is apparent from the facts given, and from the time and labor devoted to it by a large company of persons both before and after the event.

The booths varied greatly in size and design.

All were covered with white muslin as a foundation for the decorations. With this for a beginning, each lady in charge of a booth taxed her taste and skill in its adornment. The roofs, as a general thing, were made either of evergreen boughs or of tarlatan in bright tints, while the columns were wreathed with smilax, ivy geranium, and many other vines. A complete departure from this was a booth fairly embowered in pampas plumes. This was very striking. Another exception was a booth the inside walls and roof of which were solid with the feathery sprays of the graceful pepper tree. The dense green effect was relieved by the free use of spirea in bloom.

A magnificent feature of the place was the fountain, around which, in a broad ring of green turf, were imbedded the emblems of numerous societies, some being very elegant, showing exquisite taste in the selection and arrangement of the flowers. All these societies had a representative on the ground replacing each day the withered flowers in their designs with fresh ones. In close proximity to this appeared a bank of eighty thousand cut roses, a bed of eleven thousand cut calla lillies, and near at hand seven thousand pansies showed their faces—all cut from one lady's garden! Not one perished blossom was allowed to be seen in all these during the festival. There was no decrease in the supply of flowers during the entire time, and at the close of the exhibit enough were blooming in the city and country to immediately repeat the unparalleled display. Fifteen hundred fan-palm leaves—very effective in decoration—were contributed by one family.

But March 30th, the day for the festival to open, had arrived. To give the final touches to every thing during the day was an herculean task. But when the tired workers left the place for their homes, to obtain a little rest and prepare for the evening, the tabernacle presented a scene of beauty impossible for pen to describe. Now the evening has come, and what do we see? A vast mass of people so closely wedged together in the aisles and spaces, that no one can obtain any thing like a satisfactory idea of the wonderful display. Eight thousand persons, it is said, were admitted between eight and ten o'clock. The perfume from millions of flowers filled the air. So dense was the odor that breathing was difficult. A flood of electric light turned night into day. An admirably drilled band discoursed excellent music. The pretty toilets of the ladies in the long line of booths added, if possible, to the charm of the scene. The main features of the exercises were the procession through the aisles of Queen Flora and her train, her greeting to the people, and the address of the mayor of the city. The attractions of the place were maintained unabated to the final hour. Multitudes thronged the tabernacle day and evening, seeming never to tire of the beautiful scene, and always reluctant to leave.

Aside from the large pecuniary encouragement to the Festival Society, and the delight afforded to thousands of people who had never conceived of such a sight, the exhibit proved of great utility in extending the culture of the finer varieties of flowers. Indeed, the tabernacle became a grand flower exchange, in which ideas, knowledge, and experience gained in the domain of Flora, were freely communicated. Men and women, from far and near, went home to surround themselves with more beauty; to multiply their ways of doing good. Southern California immediately began to increase its stock of flowers for the next Spring's festival.

## XXXI.

## Los Angeles to San Francisco.

WE uttered our tearful farewells in the city of Los Angeles on the morning of Tuesday last, having spent one year among its remarkably sympathetic and hospitable people; a year daily brightened by touching acts of kindness performed toward us by stranger hands; a year full of obligation on our part, obligation which can never be discharged by us in other way than by holding in grateful remembrance the friends from whom we have parted.

The citizens of Los Angeles have set before them multiplied opportunities for doing good, not only in befriending strangers in health, but in soothing the last hours of dying strangers, and faithfully do many of them improve it. Could all the facts in reference to their patient and gentle care of such persons be made public, the gratitude of the whole country would be awakened, since from every quarter of the land have people gone thither in pursuit of health. Of these a large proportion are young men. Coming to the coast very ill, oftentimes without fortunes, in great need of gentle attentions, they have been received into the homes of the citizens, and by their inmates have been as assiduously nursed as if they had been brothers or sons, until the end, when they have been either gently laid to rest, or have with great painstaking been returned to their friends.

Nor is it only to the citizens of Los Angeles that this tribute of acknowledgment is due. Fifty other communities equally merit it. When in the enterprising village of Santa Ana a short time ago, several marked instances of devotion to invalid young men, by the citizens, were related to me. In one case, occurring among some Minnesota people, an outlay of nearly two hundred dollars was incurred for one sufferer's comfort, with no expectation of a return of the money.

I left Southern California with a prospect of soon emerging from its "annual panic," caused by the tardiness of the rains. This uneasiness rarely holds off until the rains are much past due. "Taking its start about the middle of Autumn, it acquires dimensions," so states a clergyman, "up to the middle of January. By that time, if the clouds have not sent down their showers, all classes of business men are at a white heat of anxiety." They well know that without rain, only partial, if any, grain crops may be expected the next year; and the crops failing, there results a general stagnation of trade. Those departments which depend much upon the daily wants of the community for support, are the best sustained, but a year of drought sadly cripples even them.

It is said that the panic—very naturally—originates with the farmers and stock-raisers. To the former, a rainless Winter signifies a direct loss in the partial if not total loss of his grain crop the next year. To the latter it means the feeding of flocks and herds from the beginning of one Winter until the middle of the next. It may also betoken the loss of large numbers of sheep and cattle by thirst and starvation. On this coast, as everywhere, these classes of producers are the fountain-head of the money resources of the country. When they lock their coffers in anticipation of a dry season, and institute a strict economy in the household, immediately the towns and cities are in trouble. Then nothing but rain can clear the sky of the future.

Probably no more rueful looking person can be seen in Southern California, while a drought is in prospect, than the owner of miles of rich grazing land, over which roam his thousands of cattle and sheep. Several such princely proprietors of real and personal property reside in the city of Los Angeles. Just before leaving there I was told that about a year ago one of these gentlemen, the owner of a celebrated ranch situated a few miles from the city, which is stocked with between thirty and forty thousand sheep, had spent the day on his domain, looking after the welfare of the animals. Returning to the city toward night, he entered his attractive home, wearing a gloomy countenance, and threw himself into an easy chair before the fire. Observing his distressed appearance, his wife inquired what was the matter.

"Wife," said he, looking up at her with an anxious face, "unless it rains to-night I shall not be worth ten cents to-morrow, for many of the sheep will die. But an all-night rain would put ten thousand dollars in my pocket."

At that moment there were some indications of a shower. The air was cold and the sky was overcast with an unbroken cloud. Before retiring, the anxious man went out to take a look at the heavens. Lo! the whole vault above him was as clear as crystal, and thickly gemmed with stars. Hope took her flight. He re-entered the house and retired, disheartened. But suddenly, a little after midnight, he heard the music of

> "Myriads of massive rain-drops,
> Falling on all around;
> Some were dancing on the house-tops,
> Some were hiding in the ground."

That was the beginning of the first heavy rain of last Winter. The proprietor of the great rancho was comforted. Of course fruit culture continues whether there be rains or not, because few vines and trees are planted without provision for irrigating them. Hence fruit crops, and the business attaching thereto, are assured, unless there come untimely frost, or unkindly insect to destroy them.

That portion of the Southern Pacific Railway which unites the cities of Los Angeles and San Francisco bears the traveler through some rare scenery. First it crosses the beautiful Valley of San Fernando, one of the finest wheat sections of Southern California; the home of the olive, fig, pear, pomegranate, and grape; a notable grazing section, and the seat of the Mission of San Fernando, the seventeenth in order of the line of missions founded by the Franciscan Fathers between San Diego and San Francisco. Of the many buildings once constituting this mission, the most interesting is the one erected as a residence for the priests. After the sequestration of the missions it was for several years the home of General Andrez Pico. Major B. C. Truman, writing of the structure, says: "It is three hundred feet long, eighty feet wide between the walls, which are four feet thick and two stories in height. The great attraction of the building is the corridor, nearly three hundred feet long, and made of columns and arches of superb masonry, with tile roof and brick floor. A vast succession of rooms compose the interior, and constitute a private residence unlike any other in America."

Drawing out from the station of San Fernando, where, on either side of the track, stood a village of white tents occupied by the Chinese railway hands, we began the ascent to the "San Fernando tunnel," six thousand nine hundred and sixty-six feet long, with a grade of one hundred feet to the mile, and requiring seven minutes for its passage. Twice that number seemed to have passed before the light broke in from the front and we dashed out upon Newhall, the shipping point for the fountains of oil concealed in the Fernando range.

Then comes the Mojave Desert, with its interesting cacti orchards, or groves of Yucca palm.

We whisked through miles of them, the trees planted, in places, with almost the regularity of orange orchards. Their clumsy limbs and bunchy foliage give them a weird appearance which allies them to a past day and a vanished people. Mojave village springs out of the hot sand, rejoices in the fervid sunlight, disdains shelter or shade, but is all alive when the trains stop for something to eat. From this point the Atlantic and Pacific Railway branches off toward the East, bearing travelers within a few miles of that masterpiece of river plowing, the cañon of the Colorado, and within easy reach of two of the largest cattle ranges on the continent.

On my return from the North two years after that, there occurred at Mojave a funny little episode which showed how necessary it is that women who travel alone should know how their tickets read. As we drew up at the place a fleshy, good-natured looking woman, seated a little back of me, arranged to take her luncheon in the cars. Procuring a small pailful of coffee from the hotel, she was soon enjoying her tempting eatables. On a track close by stood the Atlantic and Pacific train, just ready to roll out into the desert. Most of the passengers on our road had returned from dinner. At that moment, looking up in a careless way, this woman inquired if we knew of any one on the train going to St. Louis.

"Are you going to St. Louis?" asked a bright woman from Phœnix, Arizona.

"Yes."

"Does your ticket take you over the Southern Pacific? Seems to me you must change cars here. If so, that is your train; and it is about to leave."

The woman quickly opened her reticule, examined her ticket, and found to her dismay that she was booked to St. Louis, *via* the Atlantic and Pacific. Away then went her coffee. On went her bonnet. Pell-mell into its basket went her luncheon. Two ladies sprang to her side to help. One caught her wraps and umbrella. Another her satchel. The brakeman, hearing the bustle, came in and seized her pillows and blankets. Then the caravan started for the other train, stumbling over bricks and stones, and stirring up the dust. That moment the writer discovered that the woman had left her veil, seized it, ran after the others, tossed it to a man standing on the platform, and asked him to hand it to her, just as the train moved off. How she must have missed her coffee!

But northward we go, off the desert at last, and

climbing into the mountains again. Now and then we cross warm, grassy valleys, some of them threaded by little streams of water, talking gayly to the everlasting heights around. Now we are in the Soledad Cañon, thousands of feet above the sea, and climbing steadily. After awhile the hills lift up their heads grandly. Around sharp pinnacles on the left, and far above us, a snow-storm is raging, the only thing in the awful solitudes which has motion, except our steam-impelled train.

Finally, soon after dark, we gain the Tehachapi Pass, four thousand and twenty-six feet above sea level. Here the Coast Range forms a junction with the Sierra Nevada, and the result is some of the noblest scenery in California. A descent of eleven miles, and we have reached the "Loop," a bit of railroad engineering which has caused more comment than any other on the continent. And when one has studied the ground plan of the work, and understands its object, he does indeed wonder that such a plan should have been conceived for achieving such a result, on a surface of such a character.

The desire was, to carry the road out of the pass without running the track up and around the side of a steep mountain, lying in the path of the survey at the point where the loop is made, a course it would naturally take, but one involving heavy and expensive construction. To accomplish this a certain amount of vertical distance had to be overcome. To find how that could be done was the great thing. Mr. Hood, the young engineer making the survey, drew a plan by which he believed the feat could be accomplished and avoid the mountain. He submitted this to the board of directors, a board unequaled in all the history of railroad building for correct judgment and sagacity. The plan was at once adopted as by far the cheapest way out of the difficulty.

The loop is double and embraces five folds of track. To form the first loop the track makes the circuit of the base of a low butte, accomplishing a horizontal distance of three thousand seven hundred and ninety-four feet, or about three-fourths of a mile, when it plunges under itself through a tunnel four hundred and twenty-six feet long, by which a vertical distance of seventy-seven and one-half feet is overcome. The next loop increases the gain, and carries the road successfully out of the trouble. In a conversation with Mr. Hood himself on the subject, he stated that no sooner had the news of the work gone abroad than he was addressed relative to it by European engineers; and as early as two years ago two similar loops had been constructed among the mountains of the Continent. The Tehachapi loop was very easy of construction, and financially was a great success. Actual surveys show that, with all the doubling of the track, the road is only fifty feet longer than it would have been, had it been run around the mountain side.

Mr. Hood is now the chief engineer of that mighty corporation, the Southern Pacific Company. Last Spring, 1886, he was busy improving the surveys for the California and Oregon Railroad, which for many miles leads up the stupendous cañon of the Sacramento River, and after crossing some intervening rather level country, performs the feat of crossing the Siskiyou Mountains, a chain which is the peer of the Cascades in height and massiveness. How to surmount the difficulties of these great physical features must as thoroughly tax the genius of the man as did those of Tehachapi.

Our train passed over the loop about nine in the evening. At early breakfast hour next morning we were at Lathrop, where passengers take cars for Sacramento. For hours then, our route lay through the vast San Joaquin Valley. Miles of young green wheat stretched away on either side. Farmers were plowing along the way. It was December, the

Summer time of the coast. At ten o'clock we rolled into Oakland. An hour later we were in San Francisco, the metropolis of the Pacific Coast; the rival of Chicago in marvelous growth; a young city, old in wealth, institutions, commerce, railroads, and tributary towns; as cosmopolitan as New York; the gateway to the old East, to the island world of the Pacific. We spend the next year writing of its affairs, people, and surrounding country.

www.ingramcontent.com/pod-product-compliance
Lightning Source LLC
Chambersburg PA
CBHW032106220426
43664CB00008B/1153